"I love C. S. Lewis' work, and I've read many, many books about his life and writings. This book stands out to me because I believe that Lewis himself would have truly enjoyed it. It does what Lewis himself tried to do: make the most important story understandable and accessible to 'normal' people. And it does so with a winsome style that has so much in common with Lewis' own."

— BRIAN McLAREN
Author/activist (www.brianmclaren.net)

"There is a great deal written about C. S. Lewis but much of it, sadly, is hardly worth the effort. That is certainly not the case here. Original, perceptive, balanced and insightful. Essential reading for anyone concerned with Lewis and issues of faith."

— MICHAEL COREN
Author of *The Man Who Created Narnia*

"In his usual insightful way, John Bowen takes us on a romp through The Chronicles of Narnia to help us understand how Lewis' stories point us toward The Big Story that people everywhere long to hear."

— DR. HARRY L. POE
Professor of Faith and Culture, Union University

"John Bowen is a big kid, which makes him perfectly suited to write about Narnia. But this is not just a book about Narnia; it is about the spirituality of Narnia, which means it is about our world and our lives as well. John writes with the insight of a philosopher, the rigor of a historian, and the playfulness of a child. Through what feels like a kind of partnership with C. S. Lewis, John has helped me become more aware of the beauty and wonder of this world. Thank you, John, for writing this wonderful book!"

— BRUXY CAVEY
Teaching Pastor, The Meeting House (www.themeetinghouse.ca)

THE SPIRITUALITY OF NARNIA

THE SPIRITUALITY OF NARNIA

The Deeper Magic of C. S. Lewis

JOHN P. BOWEN

REGENT COLLEGE PUBLISHING
Vancouver, British Columbia

Published 2007 by
Regent College Publishing
5800 University Boulevard
Vancouver, BC v6t 2e4 Canada
Website: www.regentpublishing.com

Library and Archives Canada Cataloguing in Publication

Bowen, John P.
The spirituality of Narnia : the deeper magic of C. S. Lewis
/ John P. Bowen.

ISBN-10: 1-57383-402-5
ISBN-13: 978-1-57383-402-5

1. Lewis, C. S. (Clive Staples), 1898-1963. Chronicles of Narnia.
2. Lewis, C. S. (Clive Staples), 1898-1963—Criticism and interpretation.
3. Christian fiction, English—History and criticism. 4. Children's stories,
English—History and criticism. 5. Fantastic fiction, English—History and
criticism. 6. Spirituality in literature. I. Title.

PR6023.E926Z584 2007   823'.912   C2007-900729-5

For three friends of Narnia:

Megan Bowen
Becky Chambers
and
Sam Sumner

CONTENTS

PREFACE

I suppose I have now loved the Narnia books for half of my life. I grew up in the 1950s, when the series began to be published, and I guess they just didn't come my way during my childhood in North Wales. I forget now how I did first come across them, but I do recall a holiday in rural Yorkshire in 1976 when I read them for the first time, from start to finish, and (like so many other readers, I have discovered since) was devastated when I realized I had come to the end and there were no more. Since then, they have taken up permanent residence in my heart and imagination, their characters and incidents as important to me as things in the so-called "real" world.

One of the joys of being a friend of Narnia, of course, is introducing others to the stories. I suppose every parent who loves Narnia looks forward to reading the stories to their children, and I was no exception. I recall well the joy I felt when my firstborn, Ben, said (towards the end of the series), "Daddy, don't you think Aslan is a bit like Jesus?" My niece Megan loved the stories as a child, and I made tapes of some of the stories as birthday presents for her. Then, not long ago, I recommended Narnia to my (adult) friend Becky Chambers in England, and it was sheer delight to see her respond so intuitively to Aslan.

Some of my best memories of Narnia have to do with travel. I remember a long drive home with students from a mission trip in Northern Quebec, when Alan Bennett, Nola Crewe, Jasmine Shantz, Michael Caines and I read the stories to one another. On another drive, this time north to Sudbury in the evening, Donna Willer, Matt Adams, Marc Poitras and I took turns to read *The Horse and His Boy*, and, as our flashlight battery died, we continued reading by the light of the headlights of the car behind us. On a trip from Kenya to Tanzania, while waiting for a cell phone to be adapted to a different system, Erin Biggs and I read *The Voyage of the Dawn Treader* to one another. And my friend Rebekah Little began to read the Narnia series to her father David as he lay in hospital in the spring of 2006, preparing for the journey to Aslan's country.

Rebekah also helped me with copyright issues for this book, for which I am very grateful. I also want to thank Elin Goulden, Erin Biggs and Jeff Biggs for their superb proof-reading skills.

Narnia has helped nurture many other good friendships too: I specially appreciate Val and Kris Michaelson (and their triplets, Narnia fans all), Hal Poe, Doug Loney, Chris and Krista Dowdeswell, Donna Matheson, Allison Taylor, Erin Russell, Julie and Steve Page, and David Taylor, among others.

When I began to write this book, I was amazed at how quickly it seemed to come together. My daughter Anna shrugged and said, "Well, you've been working on it for thirty years." And I guess she was right.

The book's coming to birth, however, is more immediately due to the midwifery skills of Rob Clements, of Regent College Publishing, who told me many years ago, when he was an undergraduate at Carleton University, that he wanted to go into publishing. Little did I then know. Thanks, Rob, for believing in this project.

JOHN BOWEN
Wycliffe College, Toronto

1

LIFE, THE UNIVERSE
AND NARNIA

If you could ask God one question, what would it be? Not long ago, I sent some of my students onto the campus of the University of Toronto to ask passersby that exact question. To be honest, I was surprised by the result. I had assumed that most people would want to ask God, "Why is there evil in the world? Why so much suffering? How can you expect us to believe you are loving and yet you let these things go on?" But no: that question came in at number two. I had also expected some questions about life after death: "What happens next? Is there anything beyond the grave? Is there a heaven and a hell?" In fact, that was popular choice number three.

The question that most people wanted to ask God? "What's it all about, God? What's the meaning of life? Why are we here? Does it all mean anything?" I was surprised, though I suppose in retrospect I should not have been. It is the question which in a sense contains all the others. If we know the meaning of life, that will surely shed some light on the question of suffering. If we know what it's all about, a piece of that will probably have to do with what happens after death.

The fact that everybody asks this kind of question at one time or another probably accounts for the popularity of Douglas Adams' *Hitch-*

hiker's Guide to the Galaxy, with its ongoing search for the meaning of "Life, the Universe and Everything." But although the *Guide* is very funny (especially to those of us of British extraction, I suspect), it doesn't really offer much of an answer. Unless you count "42," the answer super-computer Deep Thought comes up with after six and a half million years. Which is funny, but not terribly helpful.

C. S. Lewis had his own struggles with life, the universe and everything. He was taken to church by his parents when he was a child, but by the age of thirteen he was a firm atheist. At this stage, he wrote to his friend Arthur Greeves to explain that he believed in no religion. None of them can be proved, he argued, and Christianity is not even the best. They are just superstitious human ideas which bring people into bondage. Lewis was just not interested.[1]

At the same time, although he was convinced that the meaning of life was not to be found in any religion, he was not closed-minded. In the same letter, he acknowledged the possibility that something could exist outside of the material world. After all, the world is very mysterious, so we cannot be absolutely certain that there is nothing more, and he wanted to welcome any "new light" that there might be on such matters.

Over the fifteen years that followed, new light dawned from several sources to make him change his mind, particularly books he read (by people like George McDonald and G. K. Chesterton) and people he met (such as J. R. R. Tolkien). He came first to believe in a supreme creator—he became a theist—almost against his will. Then, two years later, he took a further step, to become a follower of Jesus Christ, a Christian. (I will say more about Lewis' journey to Christian faith in chapter 2.)

For C. S. Lewis, Christian faith answered that most pressing of all human questions—the meaning of life—on the deepest and most comprehensive level. He then developed a passion for communicating that good news (for it *is* good news) through his speaking and his writing.

---

1.   Walter Hooper, ed. *The Letters of C. S. Lewis to Arthur Greeves 1914-1963* (New York: Harcourt Brace, 1966), 135-136.

Not that he is ever a pushy, obnoxious evangelist. He once said that of all the many different ways which exist of bringing people into God's Kingdom there were some which he specially disliked![2] Nor is he an academic theologian (though he certainly knew his theology). In fact he was suspicious, not without reason, that the formal study of theology inhibited people's ability to communicate it.[3]

No: Lewis' approach to communicating his faith is neither hard-sell nor academic. It is much more winsome. It is more along the lines of: "Let me tell you how I came to the conclusions I hold, and see if it makes sense to you"; "Let's stand side by side and look at this problem together"; and (most relevantly) "Let me tell you a story." There is a conversational, commonsense, and even narrative tone to much of his writing, as though he is writing a letter to a friend. Lots of evangelists for all sorts of causes—indeed, anyone who wants to communicate effectively—could learn from his example.

Thus one of the things Lewis is doing in The Chronicles of Narnia is sharing his faith—sharing it in a way that is engaging and interesting, a way that stirs your heart before it challenges your mind, helping you see why he thinks Christian faith makes good sense of the world. It was not the primary reason he wrote, although it was a secondary one. In fact, he tells us that his primary reason was simply that the story demanded to be told. It was as if the material for the story simply bubbled up in his mind: it was like a caged animal pawing and trying to get out. It nagged at him all day long, and got in the way of his work, his sleep and his meals. In fact, says Lewis, "It's like being in love.[4]

---

2. "Cross-Examination," in C. S. Lewis, *God in the Dock: Essays on Theology and Ethics* (Grand Rapids: Eerdmans 1970), 262.

3. He thought candidates for ordained office should have to sit a compulsory exam to see if they could communicate their faith in language ordinary people would understand. If they failed that exam, they could not become pastors, however brilliantly they performed in their other exams. "Letter to 'The Christian Century,'" December 31, 1958, in *God in the Dock*, 338.

4. "Sometimes Fairy Stories May Say Best What's to be Said," in Walter Hooper, ed. *Of This and Other Worlds* (London: Collins, 1982), 72.

But as the stories unfolded, it became clear to him (and to his readers) that actually he was communicating certain distinctive beliefs about the world. He is not going to hit you over the head with his beliefs—if you have read the books, you will know that he does not do that—but his hope is that if you enjoy the stories, you will want to know more about the beliefs that inspired them.

How do stories connect with beliefs? After all, they often seem like different things: philosophy and novels are found in quite different parts of the library. One way they are linked is simply this—that our stories shape our beliefs.

When I say our stories shape our beliefs, we don't need to look in the first place to fiction. For example, the stories we hear told in our families as we are growing up shape our minds and hearts and convictions before we are ever aware that they are doing so. Perhaps they are stories about how our family came to Canada—out of persecution or hardship or heroism. And so we absorb the belief that evil can be turned into good with courage and hard work. Not because anyone ever explicitly put it that way, but just because that's the outlook the stories shaped in us.

The converse is also true: Our beliefs shape the stories we want to hear and the stories we want to read to our children. For example, we no longer tell stories about how brave knights on horseback rescue fair but helpless damsels in distress and sweep them away to a happily-ever-after wedding. Such depictions do not express our culture's convictions about how the sexes relate (or should relate). We want our daughters to read stories about girls who are resourceful and energetic, not passive and dependent. We want our sons to hear stories that show girls being just as strong and brave as they are. So we discard the old stories and write ourselves new ones.

Of course, this is a circular process, since the beliefs we express in our stories also have to come from somewhere, and that is likely to be yet another story. These days, of course, these stories are more likely to be written not in the language of knights and damsels but the language of socio-psycho-biology and gender politics. But they are still stories which shape our minds and our hearts. Once again story and conviction intertwine.

This being so, it is impossible to ask which comes first, the story or the belief. Each feeds the other. But it is important to recognize the connection. Stories are never value-free and beliefs are never just abstract propositions.

Let's move beyond family mythologies, children's fairy tales and scientific explanations. Somewhere along the way, we also pick up bigger stories, not just about our families, our country and our gender, but about Life, the Universe and Everything. These are stories about where the world came from and where it is going, who human beings are and what they are for, about the problems of the world and their solution. These stories too shape our convictions and are shaped by our convictions. They may inspire us, discourage us, or puzzle us. If my students' informal survey is anything to go by, those stories often leave us dissatisfied and wondering if there is a more satisfying story to be found somewhere.

Some of these stories are very optimistic. For example, there is a popular one that goes like this: Once upon a time, the universe began with a Big Bang. Then much later on, life began, at first very simply but with increasing complexity, until evolution produced human beings. Over time, human beings are learning how to live wisely and successfully on this fragile planet, and, if we are successful, there is no reason we could not find a way to colonize other planets before our sun cools down and dies. Not that that offers much comfort to individuals in the here and now, of course. (As it happens, C. S. Lewis found this view unbelievable, and parodied it in his science fiction trilogy.)

Some stories are more consistently gloomy. In spite of the zany humour, the big story underlying *The Hitchhiker's Guide* is actually a deeply pessimistic, even nihilistic, one. There is no god (the man who rules the universe is senile, lives in a leaky hut, and calls his cat "the Lord"), the meaning of life is 42 (which helps no-one), events happen randomly and without meaning (often because of advanced but faulty technology), and when the prophet Zarquon returns at the end of time (as his followers always believed he would), he is a doddery old man who has no idea what is going on.

Most who have a hopeless view like this find some spark of hope, perhaps in the experience of love. But in *The Hitchhiker's Guide*, though love can be wonderful, it comes rarely and briefly. The hero, Arthur Dent, does not find true love until the fourth book of the "trilogy," when he falls in love with a woman bearing the unlikely name of Fenchurch. Before long, however, he is separated from her (through a random technological accident, naturally) and never finds her again. As you might expect, the trilogy has no happy ending. For some readers, this undoubtedly confirms the suspicions they already had about the nature of the universe.

The Hitchhiker's Guide is a good example of how writers' personal beliefs about the story of the universe spill over into the stories that they write, and in turn help to shape or reinforce our own convictions. This is only to be expected. Who we are, what we believe and what we create are all bound up together. To try and separate them out would be like trying to unscramble an egg. Every work of art carries the artist's signature, whether the artist intends it or not. So our little stories—novels, family mythology, children's fairy stories—unless we deliberately choose otherwise, will reflect our understanding of the Big Story.

So with the Narnia stories. Into the particulars of the individual stories—whether of Edmund or Eustace, Caspian or Lucy, Puddleglum or Reepicheep, Aravis or Puzzle—are woven the melodies of what Lewis believed was the symphony of the universe. And as we are drawn into the adventures, we are unconsciously learning not only how Lewis views the world of Narnia, but how he viewed our world. And our own view of the world is shaped, or affirmed, or challenged, as a result.

Wordsworth once wrote, "We murder to dissect," meaning, when we take something to pieces, we lose something of its reality and vitality. I think he is wrong, because my plan is to "dissect" the Narnia stories—to show the Story that underlies the stories—not in order to murder them but with the hope of deepening your delight in them. The statement that God is "a hedonist at heart" is found on the lips of Lewis' demonic character Screwtape[5], but is nevertheless true to Lewis' convictions. Lewis believed that God's purpose for the world can be summed up in the one word *joy*. In heaven, he says, we will get to drink joy from the fountain of joy.[6] The purpose of the Narnia stories was also to bring joy—and it would be perverse of me to want to do anything less than enhance that joy.

How may we unravel the different strands, the various melodies, of the Narnia stories? I suggested earlier that our Big Stories tell us where the world came from and where it is going, who we are and why we are here. My plan is to tease out how the Narnian Chronicles address such questions. Two friends of mine have written a whole book about how one can think about and compare different Stories, and they suggest that there are four particularly useful questions one can ask of any story. Let me tell you the questions and show how I think they are helpful in understanding the Big Story of Narnia.[7]

• *Where are we?* What kind of a world is Narnia? Is this a good place to be or a scary place? A world made by a god (either nice or nasty), or a world that just happened by chance? Does this world have any importance to anyone except its inhabitants? Or are we simply, as Douglas Adams expresses it, "[f]ar out in the uncharted backwaters of the unfashionable end of the Western Spiral arm of the Galaxy"?[8]

• *Who are we?* Who are the inhabitants of Narnia? What do we know about them? Do they have value? Or are they meaningless flukes of nature?

---

5. C.S. Lewis, *The Screwtape Letters* (London: Geoffrey Bles, 1942; Reprint, Fontana, 1977), 127.

6. "The Weight of Glory," in *Screwtape Proposes a Toast and Other Pieces* (London: Fontana Books, 1965), 108.

7. Brian Walsh and Richard Middleton, *The Transforming Vision: Shaping a Christian Worldview* (Downers Grove: InterVarsity Press, 1984), 35. They use the language of worldviews and metanarratives, but it basically means the same as the language of Big Stories, which seems more appropriate when talking about Narnia.

8. *The Hitchhiker's Guide to the Galaxy*, 5.

• *What is the problem?* What is fundamentally wrong in Narnia? What are the symptoms and what is the cause?

• *What is the solution?* Is there any chance the problem can be put right? And who is there who is capable of doing it?

To these four, I would like to add a fifth question which (to my mind anyway) highlights a further dimension of any story:

• *Where are we going?* What is the ultimate fate of Narnia and its inhabitants, and how does that affect things in the present?

These questions will guide us in unearthing the convictions of C. S. Lewis and help us understand what it was that so captured Lewis' own heart and mind. And maybe in that way he can help us think more clearly about our own understanding of The Big Story.

Before beginning on that journey, however, it will prepare the ground if we look at the dual origins of the world of Narnia—Aslan, in one sense the creator of Narnia, and C. S. Lewis himself, the "sub-creator" (to use Tolkien's word[9]) of Narnia.

---

9.   J. R. R. Tolkien. "On Fairy Stories," in *Tree and Leaf* (London: George Allen and Unwin, 1968), 49.

2

WHO WAS C.S. LEWIS?

C.S. Lewis is one of the most unlikely children's authors you could ever meet. He was a university professor all of his working life, first at Oxford and later at Cambridge. He was not married till he was over fifty, and had no children of his own, nor any nephews or nieces. His closest friends were other male academics. His favourite pastimes were walking in the country and talking about books. He fought in France in the First World War and went on holiday to Greece towards the end of his life, but apart from that did not travel outside the British Isles. Lewis described himself thus:

> I am tall, fat, rather bald, red-faced, double-chinned, black-haired, have a deep voice, and wear glasses for reading.[1]

1.　C.S. Lewis, *Letters to Children.* Lyle Dorsett and Marjorie Lamp Mead, Eds. (Toronto: Simon and Schuster, 1985), 45. One writer notes, "Kenneth Tynan said Lewis combined the manner of Friar Tuck with the mind of St. Augustine" (Corbin Scott Carnell, *Bright Shadow of Reality: Spiritual Longing in C.S. Lewis* [Grand Rapids: Eerdmans, 1974], 32). Tolkien told Neville Coghill that he modelled the voice of Treebeard in *The Lord of the Rings* on that of *C.S. Lewis.* Humphrey Carpenter, *J.R.R. Tolkien: A Biography* (London: Allen and Unwin, 1978), 198.

And he dressed in the manner of a typical absent-minded professor, in baggy pants and tweed jackets.[2] How could such a person write successful children's books? Over the fifty or so years since the Narnia stories began to appear, around 100 million copies have been sold. So what do we know about this man, C. S. Lewis?

Part of me does not want to write this chapter, simply because I am not sure Lewis would want a chapter entitled "Who was C. S. Lewis?" I think this because, in the 1930s, he had an extended debate with E. M. W. Tillyard, another Oxford professor, about whether knowing an author's biography helped or hindered an appreciation of the author's work. Lewis thought that, on balance, the biography was irrelevant, and could even hinder one's enjoyment.[3] A book needs to stand on its own feet as a work of art, and be assessed and responded to without any outside influence—even that of the author's life.

There is another, related reason for my reluctance. Lewis wrote an essay entitled "Meditation in a Woodshed."[4] He was standing in his woodshed one sunny afternoon, and noticed that, when the door was shut, he could see the specks of dust dancing in the sunlight. Then he looked at the crack above the door through which the light was shining, and realized that by means of that same beam of light, he could see the world outside the shed. This led him to reflect on two ways of seeing—looking directly at a thing, and looking along it in order to see what it illuminates. What I am planning to do by looking at the spirituality of Narnia is not so much to look at C. S. Lewis, but to look in the same direction as he looked, to try and see what he saw and why he saw it—if you like, to look *along* the light of C. S. Lewis, not *at* it.

So why this chapter? I think there is in most of us a curiosity about the lives of creative artists. Maybe we want to know something of how they were able to do what they did. What was their inspiration?

---

2. Humphrey Carpenter *The Inklings* (London: Allen and Unwin, 1978), 38.

3. The exchange was later published as *The Personal Heresy: A Controversy*, by E. M. W. Tillyard and C. S. Lewis (Oxford University Press, 1939).

4. *God in the Dock*, 212.

Where did they get their ideas from? Perhaps we hope that knowing such things will stimulate our own creativity. Certainly people asked Lewis such questions—more than one of his *Letters to Children* deal with this issue—and I am encouraged to find that he answered more patiently than his argument with Tillyard might lead one to expect. And, of course, he did write a slim volume of autobiography, *Surprised by Joy*, specifically because people wanted to know more of the person whose books they loved. As he explained in the preface, "This book is written partly in answer to requests that I would tell how I passed from Atheism to Christianity."[5] Naturally, if you agree with Lewis in his argument with Tillyard, you can simply skip to the next chapter.

So, to return to the original question: who was C.S. Lewis? Clive Staples Lewis was born on November 29, 1898, outside Belfast, in Northern Ireland. His father Albert was a lawyer. His mother Flora was daughter of an Anglican minister, and (unusually for those days) graduated from university in Belfast. At the age of four, Lewis announced that henceforth he would answer only to the name of Jacksie, which in time became shortened to Jack, the name by which he was known for the rest of his life. He and his older brother Warren (known as Warnie) became and remained best friends.

He had exposure to the Anglican church, but it made little impact on him:

> I was taught the usual things and made to say my prayers and in
> due time taken to church. I naturally accepted what I was told but I
> cannot remember feeling much interest in it.[6]

The family went to the church where his grandfather was the minister and preacher. There were two things he particularly disliked at church. Firstly, the preaching was emotional, and therefore embarrassing to a small boy, and its main theme was the (supposed) evils of Roman

---

5.   *Surprised by Joy* (London: Geoffrey Bles, 1955), 7.
6.   Ibid., 12.

Catholicism. Secondly, he came to suspect that people's attendance was for political more than spiritual reasons: to be Anglican was socially acceptable, whereas to be Catholic was not.[7]

When Jack was seven years old, his family moved to Little Lea, a large rambling house with an attic and the "Little End Room" which became the boys' retreat. During that period, he observed later, he lived "almost entirely in [his] imagination."[8] From the nursery, they could look out on the Castlereagh Hills, a mile away, and Lewis felt for the first time that sense of mystery and longing which he was later to describe as "joy."[9] Around this time, there were other experiences of this kind of joy—through a toy garden Warnie created, and through the children's books of Beatrix Potter. Perhaps most significantly, however, he was captivated by reading a translation of an ancient Norse myth, "Tegner's Drapa."[10] Struggling to convey that early experience of joy, Lewis says in his autobiography that he "desired with almost sickening intensity something never to be described."[11] Since this feeling was triggered by stories from Scandinavia, he dubbed it an experience of "Northernness." Even though at the time these were simply delightful feelings, these experiences were to prove highly significant in his spiritual development. Indeed, he commented that "the central story of my life is about nothing else."[12] Much further down the road, the experience of joy was to become a central motif of the Narnia Chronicles.

7.   Warren Hamilton Lewis, *C. S. Lewis: A Biography* (unpublished typescript in the Wade Collection, Wheaton), 232, in *Jack*, 217-218.

8.   *Surprised by Joy*, 18.

9.   Ibid., 12.

10.   Esias Tegner was a nineteenth-century Swedish poet who wrote a "drapa" (a kind of Old Norse poem) about the death of the Norse god Balder. What Lewis read was a translation of this poem by English poet Henry Wadsworth Longfellow.

11.   *Surprised by Joy*, 19-20.

12.   Ibid., 20.

Then, in 1908, his mother died of cancer. Jack was devastated: "all settled happiness . . . disappeared from my life."[13] His father, not knowing what else to do, sent Jack within a month to the same boarding school Warren had gone to the previous year. The school was so bad that he refers to it as "Belsen" (the name of a Second World War concentration camp). After two years there, he transferred for one semester to a school nearer home, then to Cherbourg, a "prep school" that prepared boys for entrance into Malvern College at the age of fourteen or fifteen.

At the first school, the religious instruction emphasized the reality of hell (he says "I feared for my soul"[14]), but obviously didn't tell him how to avoid it. At Cherbourg, he tried to learn to pray but found he became obsessively introspective about whether he was doing it "right." "Had I pursued the same road much further," he comments, "I think I should have gone mad."[15] Looking back, he called it "the dry husks of Christianity," not the real thing. He was eleven years old.

During this time, he did well academically, well enough to win a scholarship to a private school called Malvern, where he studied for one year. By this time, however, his experiences of joy had been long forgotten, until one day he accidentally discovered the music of the nineteenth-century romantic composer Wagner[16] and the illustrations of Arthur Rackham.[17] At once, his feeling for "Northernness" returned.

---

13.   Ibid., 23.

14.   Ibid., 33.

15.   Ibid., 54.

16.   Wilhelm Richard Wagner (1813-1883). Wagner's compositions have been a strong influence on many 20th century film scores, notably John Williams' music for *Star Wars*.

17.   Arthur Rackham (1867-1939) was an English book illustrator. Although he is best known for illustrating children's books such as *Rip van Winkle* (1905), *Peter Pan* (1906) and *Alice in Wonderland* (1907), he also illustrated numerous books for adult readers such as *The Rhinegold and the Valkyrie* (1911) .

Although in retrospect he recognized his feeling for joy and Northernness as a deep spiritual longing, at the time he made no connection between them and his experience of Christianity to date. Quite the contrary. He later realized that Northernness gave him something which his religion should have provided but did not[18]—particularly the beauty, mystery and sense of longing he experienced in the old sagas. Mythology became almost a substitute religion for him. He felt reverence towards the gods of Norse mythology that he later realized should be given to God—but he had never felt that in church. Not surprisingly, at Cherbourg Lewis found he "was desperately anxious to get rid of [his] religion"[19] and was relieved to find a way of escape. At the age of thirteen, he declared himself an atheist.

Around this time, he met a boy of his own age in Belfast named Arthur Greeves. Lewis called Arthur his "First Friend" because what immediately connected them was a love of Northernness. In *The Four Loves,* Lewis describes a friend as someone who cares about the same truth that you do.[20] Arthur never left Belfast, but (partly as a result) became one of Lewis' most regular and lifelong correspondents, and it was to Arthur that the letters were written which spelled out his gradual move from atheism to Christianity.

After hearing Jack's complaints about school, his father decided to send him to study with W. T. Kirkpatrick, the headmaster of the school he, Albert, had gone to. He was known as "the Great Knock," and was now living in retirement in Surrey, in the south of England. Two and a half years with Kirkpatrick, a rigorous rationalist and atheist, finally provided Lewis with the environment in which he could begin to develop his intellectual potential. Here he learned Latin and Greek, French and Italian, and the joy of intellectual thrust and parry. This period, he said,

---

18.   Roger Lancelyn Green and Walter Hooper, *C.S. Lewis: A Biography* (New York: Harcourt Brace, 1974) 33, cf. Carnell, *Bright Shadow of Reality*, 42.

19.   *Surprised by Joy*, 53.

20.   *The Four Loves*, 62.

was like "red beef and strong beer"[21] and in *Miracles,* one of Lewis' early books, he acknowledges "an immense debt" to Kirkpatrick.[22] Kirkpatrick, not one given to ready praise, wrote to Lewis' father that "His reasoning capacity is beyond his years."[23]

During this time, however, the two halves of his brain—the intellectual and the imaginative—continued to exist in separate solitudes, the former stimulated by Kirkpatrick, the latter not at all.[24] In particular, rationalism did not help him make sense of the experience of joy:

> The two hemispheres of my mind were in sharpest contrast. On
> the one side a many-islanded sea of poetry and myth; on the other
> a glib and shallow "rationalism." Nearly all that I loved I believed to
> be imaginary; nearly all that I believed to be real I thought grim and
> meaningless.[25]

At about this time, Lewis discovered a book entitled *Phantastes* by George McDonald (1824-1905), the first of several authors who would begin to open his mind to a new way of thinking about Christianity.[26] MacDonald was a Scottish minister who, having been turned off by the rigid dogmatism he encountered at seminary, turned to children's literature as a means of conveying spiritual truths. Lewis would later call him his "master," commenting that he knew "hardly any other writer who seems to be closer, or more continually close, to the Spirit of Christ Himself."[27]

---

21.   *Surprised by Joy,* 111.

22.   C.S. Lewis, *Miracles, A Preliminary Study* (London: Geoffrey Bles, 1947), 73..

23.   Clive Hamilton [C.S. Lewis], *Spirits in Bondgae: A Cycle of Lyrics* (London: Heinemann, 1919), xxiii.

24.   *Surprised by Joy,* 138.

25.   Ibid., 138.

26.   McDonald's influence is reflected in the fact that Lewis later made him his guide to heaven and hell in *The Great Divorce* (London: Geoffrey Bles, 1945; Reprint, New York: HarperCollins, 1977).

27.   For a helpful introduction to the life and writings of George MacDonald, see Rolland Hein's anthology, *The Heart of George MacDonald* (Vancouver, B.C.: Regent

While in hospital in France a couple of years later, he read a book by G. K. Chesterton (1874-1936), a Roman Catholic writer, whose humor and goodness Lewis appreciated. In *Surprised by Joy,* he reflects ruefully, "A young man who wishes to remain a sound Atheist cannot be too careful of his reading. There are traps everywhere."[28]

Just before Christmas 1916, Lewis took the entrance exam to University College in Oxford, and as a result was awarded a scholarship to study Classics. (Lewis had no problem with the exam, except for the math part, which he failed. Fortunately, because allowances were made for returning service men, he never had to retake it.) In 1914 England had declared war on Germany, and in 1917, like other Oxford students, Lewis was expected to join the Officers Training Corps. Here he found himself sharing a room with a young man named Paddy Moore, and through him met Paddy's mother Janie. Lewis promised Paddy that should anything happen to him (Moore), he (Lewis) would take care of Janie.

Lewis went to France, was wounded in action, and shortly afterwards returned to England. Around the same time, the news came that Paddy had been killed. Lewis returned to Oxford in January 1919 and in April of that year Janie moved there too. When in his second year he was allowed to live outside the college, he moved in with Mrs. Moore and her fourteen-year-old daughter, Maureen. There has been some debate as to whether the relationship between Jack and Janie was a sexual one, since she was twenty-six years older than he. However, A. N. Wilson, one of Lewis' biographers, has pointed out that "Neither of them was a Christian, nor were they bound by any code of morality which would have forbidden them to become lovers in the fullest sense of the word."[29] They continued to share a home until Mrs. Moore's death in 1951, though it seems likely that their sexual relationship (if there was one) came to an end at the latest when Lewis became a Christian in 1931. Nine years after

---

College Publishing, 2004).

28.   *Ibid.,* 153-154.

29.   A. N. Wilson, *C. S. Lewis: A Biography* (London: Collins, 1990), 58.

her death, in *Surprised by Joy*, Lewis refers to the relationship simply as "one huge and complex episode" and says no more.[30]

He received his Classics degree, with First Class Honours, in 1922. Because of the poor job market in classics, however, he was advised to take a second B.A., and this he did in a single year, again taking First Class Honours in English.

During this time he made friends with a fellow student named Owen Barfield, who caused him to reconsider his views about the reality of the supernatural. Barfield was for Lewis the "Second Friend," someone who cared about the right questions, but came to the wrong conclusions: "he has read all the right books but has got the wrong thing out of every one."[31]

He also met scholars Neville Coghill, Hugo Dyson, and J.R.R. Tolkien, all of whom, to Lewis' shock, turned out to be Christians. The spiritual influences on Jack were increasing in number. As he wrote later, "The great Angler played his fish and I never dreamed that the hook was in my tongue."[32]

The year after he finished his studies was a frustrating and stressful one in that Lewis could not find suitable work. Finally, he got a one-year appointment as a philosophy tutor at University College (the Oxford college from which he had graduated). This was followed by his winning a fellowship (the equivalent of tenure) at Magdalen College.

North Americans are surprised to learn that, although he had two first degrees, he had no earned master's degree and no doctorate, and (upon his appointment) he had published nothing of an academic nature. He remained at Magdalen until 1954, when he became a professor at Cambridge.

Spiritually, however, he was still confused. On the one hand, his atheism had no place for the life of the imagination or for his experience of joy. On the other hand, he was slowly learning through books

---

30. *Surprised by Joy,* 160.
31. Ibid., 161.
32. Ibid., 169.

and friends a very different understanding of Christianity from the one he had rejected years before. In 1926, he was impressed by reading Chesterton's *The Everlasting Man,* which made him think "Chesterton the most sensible man alive 'apart from his Christianity'."[33] His faith was further shaken when an atheist colleague suggested that the biographies of Jesus, the Gospels, might be historically true.[34]

He describes a moment of choice while riding the bus up Headington Hill in Oxford. He became aware of a growing spiritual pressure on him, and realized that he was "shutting something out." In a sense he didn't do anything, but he chose to stop resisting, and (using an image that would recur in *The Lion, the Witch and the Wardrobe*) felt like "a man of snow at long last beginning to melt."[35]

By his own accounting, however, he did not actually acknowledge the reality of God until the spring of 1929, when he "admitted that God was God" and became "the most reluctant and dejected convert in all England."[36] It is as though he did not want to believe; he was not excited, there was no ecstasy and no vision. He makes his experience sound more like that of someone who says, "Oh well, I guess two and two really do have to make four." He was still not a Christian—but this was a significant step in that direction.

The transition from theism to Christianity was finally precipitated on September 19, 1931, by a late-night conversation with his friends J. R. R. Tolkien and Hugo Dyson. As they walked in Addison's Walk, behind Magdalen, they discussed myth.[37] For Lewis, up to this point, the stories of Jesus, the God who dies and rises again, were simply another form of

---

33. *Surprised by Joy,* 178.

34. Ibid., 178-179.

35. Ibid.

36. Ibid., 182.

37. Lewis' poem, "What the Bird Said Early in the Year," with its moving conclusion, "Quick, quick, quick, quick, the gates are drawn apart" is now engraved on a stone at the entrance to Addison's Walk.

a timeless myth, and not to be taken seriously.[38] Tolkien (following Chesterton) argued that, in Jesus, myth actually broke into history, and so it is hardly surprising that mythologies in many cultures should prefigure the actual event. The mythologies of the world are preparing the way for the reality.

For Jack, this was a crucial connection. How to put together the life of the intellect and the passion of the imagination had been a lifelong puzzle, and now, to his surprise, the key appeared to be in the very Christian faith he had once rejected. He explained his discovery to Arthur shortly afterwards by saying that "the story of Christ is simply a true myth." Other myths are human inventions, not tied to a particular place or time. But in Christianity, that myth breaks through into the world of space and time—a little town called Bethlehem in the reign of Augustus Caesar. The Christian story "is God's myth."[39]

The final stage of his conversion took place three days later as he rode with Warnie to Whipsnade Zoo, halfway between Oxford and Cambridge. "When we set out," he wrote, "I did not believe that Jesus Christ is the Son of God, and when we reached the zoo I did."[40] Again, the experience was not dramatic: it didn't have to be. "It was more like, when a man, after long sleep, still lying motionless in bed, becomes aware that he is now awake."[41]

Then began a flow of books, both academic and theological, at a rate of roughly one each year for the rest of Lewis' life. A group of literary friends known as "the Inklings" gathered around Lewis. They would meet in Lewis' rooms at Magdalen every Thursday evening to read and discuss whatever they were writing at the time. In this way, the Inklings were the first to hear *The Lord of the Rings* (which is dedicated to them)

---

38. An attempt to revive this argument has recently been made by Tom Harpur in *The Pagan Christ* (Toronto: Thomas Allen, 2005).

39. *The Letters of C. S. Lewis to Arthur Greaves*, October 18th, 1931. Cf., "Myth Became Fact" in *God in the Dock*, 166.

40. *Surprised by Joy*, 189.

41. Ibid.

as well as *The Screwtape Letters, The Problem of Pain* (also dedicated to the Inklings) and others of Lewis' books. Some of the Inklings met on a Tuesday morning at a pub in downtown Oxford called the Eagle and Child. The Thursday meetings came to an end in 1949, but the pub meetings continued till the end of Lewis' life.

One late but influential addition to the group was Charles Williams (1886-1945), who worked for Oxford University Press. Between 1939 and Williams' untimely death in 1945, Williams helped Lewis grasp that Christian faith was more multi-dimensional than pure rationalism would allow. Among other things, he teased Lewis that Job's comforters were "the sort of people who write books on the Problem of Pain."[42] The influence of Williams is indicated by the fact that, when Lewis published *That Hideous Strength* in 1945, some called it "a Charles Williams novel by C. S. Lewis."[43]

During the war years, Lewis contributed to Britain's "war effort" by agreeing to give a series of lectures to members of the Royal Air Force. He did not feel they were very effective. Indeed, he wrote to his friend Sister Penelope: "as far as I can judge they were a complete failure."[44] In fact, he learned some things about communicating with non-academic folk, and out of these lectures came the talks later broadcast on the BBC and eventually (in 1952) combined into one of his most popular books, *Mere Christianity.*

During the war, he also had "evacuees" to stay at The Kilns, his home in Oxford. These were children who had been shipped out of London and other major cities to escape the possible dangers of the war. George

---

42.   Lewis' Preface to *Essays Presented to Charles Williams*, xiii, cited in Carnell, 63.

43.   Joe R. Christopher, "Charles Walter Stanley Williams," in Jeffrey D. Schultz and John G. West, Jr., eds. *The C. S. Lewis Readers' Encyclopedia*. (Grand Rapids: Zondervan, 1998), 427..

44.   Walter Hooper, ed., *The Collected Letters of C. S. Lewis*, Vol. II (New York: HarperCollins, 2004), May 15, 1941. Sister Penelope was a member of the Sisters of the Community of St. Mary the Virgin in Wantage. She wrote to him in August 1939 praising *Out of the Silent Planet* and they corresponded for the rest of Lewis' life. *Perelandra* is dedicated to the sisters ("To some Ladies at Wantage").

Sayer sees a direct connection between this and the origins of the Chronicles:

> The evacuated children staying at the Kilns provided the original inspiration. One of them showed an interest in an old wardrobe, asking if she could go inside and if there was anything behind it .... Now he thought of writing a story for and about the evacuated children.[45]

The wardrobe is not the only connection with the evacuees: as *The Lion, the Witch and the Wardrobe* begins, the Pevensie children themselves are evacuees, "sent away from London during the war because of the air-raids."[46] After a flurry of other books, *The Lion, the Witch and the Wardrobe* was published in 1950, and after that a new Narnia story appeared almost every year. Tolkien disapproved deeply of the series, feeling that "Lewis had written them too quickly, that they were inconsistent in detail, and that they were unconvincing in their picture of a 'secondary world'"—not accusations that could be made of *The Lord of the Rings*, which Lewis considered "almost unequalled in the whole range of narrative art."[47]

In 1950, Lewis began to correspond with an American woman named Joy Gresham, who came to visit him in Oxford. After a divorce in 1953, Joy returned to England, this time to London with her sons, David and Douglas. In 1954, he dedicated *The Horse and His Boy* to the boys. Jack and Joy spent time together (not least working on his new novel, *Till We Have Faces,* which he considered "far and away the best I have written"[48]), and in 1955, she and the boys moved to Oxford.

---

45.   George Sayer, *Jack: A Life of C. S. Lewis* (New York: Harper & Row, 1988; Reprint, Wheaton: Crossway Books, 1994), 311.

46.   C.S. Lewis, *The Lion, the Witch and the Wardrobe* (London: Geoffrey Bles, 1950; Reprint, London: HarperCollins, 1980), 9.

47.   "J.R.R.Tolkien" in Schulz and West, 406.

48.   *Letters of C. S. Lewis,* ed. W. H. Lewis (New York: Harcourt Brace, 1966), 492.

In that same year, Jack had been offered, and accepted, a professorship created with him in mind at Cambridge. He had been increasingly unhappy with his work at Oxford, and there was no prospect of promotion there, quite possibly because of his public Christian stand. As a result, he accepted the new position with the condition that he should continue to live in Oxford but stay in Cambridge from Monday to Friday.

In the spring of 1956, he married Joy in a registry office wedding, a formality Lewis regarded as "a pure matter of friendship and expediency . . . simply a legal form"[49] so that she (an American citizen) could legally continue to live in England. Shortly after this, however, she was diagnosed with bone cancer, causing Lewis to realize that he really did love her and wanted a "proper" wedding, which took place in Joy's hospital room. She was then moved to The Kilns, supposedly to die, but experienced an almost miraculous recovery. She remained in remission for eighteen months, during which time they had holidays in Ireland and Greece together, but the cancer then returned, and she died in the summer of 1960.

By 1961, Lewis' own health was failing, and, though he continued to write, he knew he had not long to live. In September 1963, he wrote to a friend, "My last fear has been taken from me. . . . It is all rather fun—solemn fun—isn't it?"[50] He died at his home on November 22, 1963, the same day that President John F. Kennedy was shot. Lewis was buried in the churchyard of Headington Parish Church, where he had worshiped since his conversion thirty years before.

Kierkegaard said that life is only understood in retrospect. It is perhaps whimsical to suggest that Lewis' life can be read as leading inevitably to the writing of the Narnia books. Nevertheless, his childhood imagination and reading; his mysterious experiences of joy from an early age; his rejection of a religion that had no place for joy or the imagination; his slow discovery of a faith that was different; then his learning how to

---

49.　　Green and Hooper, 268.

50.　　Ibid., 304-305.

express that faith in ways that were imaginative as well as rational: all of these factors seem to flow together to create the Chronicles.

It is almost as if an invisible hand were helping to shape the imagination of C. S. Lewis so that he in turn could shape the stories. Certainly Lewis' friend Tolkien had that sense about his own work. Writing about the climax of *The Lord of the Rings,* he says: "The Other Power then took over: the Writer of the Story (by which I do not mean myself)."[51]

Perhaps Tolkien and Lewis talked together about this sense that more was involved in their writing than just their own efforts. Whether or not that is the case (and I for one would like to think it was), Tolkien certainly understood his creative role as that of a "sub-creator," imitating on a small scale the work of the Creator of the universe.

If Lewis is only the sub-creator of Narnia, there is a certain irony in the fact that one of the characters he created is the "true" creator of Narnia, the lion Aslan. It is to Aslan that we now turn.

---

51.   H. Carpenter with C. Tolkien, eds. *The Letters of J. R. R. Tolkien* (Boston: Houghton Mifflin, 1981), 252-253.

3

ASLAN'S OTHER NAME

The main character in all of the Narnia stories is a lion named Aslan. As Lewis tried to reconstruct what had happened in the creative process leading up to the writing of the books, it was the lion who provided the unifying factor for all the scattered ideas he had. When asked how he came to write *The Lion, the Witch and the Wardrobe*, for example, he said that he had little idea of how the story would go until the figure of "Aslan came bounding into it." He quickly became the focal point, and "soon He pulled the six other Narnian stories in after Him."[1]

So who is Aslan? I hesitate to name him, and will not often do so in the chapters that follow, for fear of breaking the spell of the books. But outside the Chronicles, Lewis himself does talk about the identity of Aslan, so I will cautiously follow his lead in this. In his *Letters to Children*, in particular, he names Aslan even though at times he is a little reluctant to do so. Often Lewis gives us some broad hints without being explicit. For example, at the end of *The Voyage of the Dawn*

---

1. "It All Began With a Picture" in C. S. Lewis, *Of This and Other Worlds*, ed. Walter Hooper (London: Collins Fount Paperbacks, 1982), 79.

Treader, Aslan says he has "another name" in our world.[2] One child, a girl named Hila, has obviously asked Lewis about Aslan's mysterious other name. Lewis replies, "I want you to guess." He asks her to see if she can think of someone who (like Aslan) arrived in our world at the same time as Santa Claus, said he was the son of the Emperor, was killed for someone else's fault, came back to life, and is sometimes referred to as a lamb. He concludes, "Don't you really know His name in this world. Think it over and let me know your answer!"[3]

For children who have grown up with some knowledge of the stories of Jesus (as would have been common in England and North America in the 1950s), these hints should have made the answer perfectly obvious.

In fact, Lewis comments later, in the last letter he ever wrote, that it was usually the children who recognized the identity of Aslan, while adults did not.[4] Perhaps it is because children do identify Aslan with Jesus that in many of his letters Lewis does not hide the truth. Indeed, more than once he refers to the presence of Aslan (rather than Jesus) at work in his own life. He tells one child of Joy's illness and of the possibility of her death (going to Aslan's country), but adds that "I am sure Aslan knows best and . . . He will do what is right."[5]

Then, later that year, he wrote to the same child to report on Joy's miraculous recovery and says: "Aslan has done great things for us."[6] For him, obviously, there is an open door between Narnia and our world, and Aslan passes back and forth between the two, known there only as Aslan, but here by either name.

Within the Narnia stories themselves, there are hints that Aslan is Jesus in a different form. In another letter to a child, Lewis tells us that we should look for these clues "[a]t the v.[ery] edge of the Narnian

2.   C.S. Lewis, *The Voyage of the Dawn Treader* (London: Geoffrey Bles, 1955; Reprint, London: HarperCollins, 1980), 209.

3.   *Letters to Children,* 32.

4.   Ibid., 114.

5.   Ibid., 69.

6.   Ibid., 76.

world" because that is where Aslan begins to appear more like Christ as we know him in our world.[7] The edge of Narnia is found in two stories—*The Voyage of the Dawn Treader*, where the children come to the boundary of Aslan's country, and *The Last Battle*, where they finally find themselves living in Aslan's land, and "as He[8] spoke He no longer looked to them like a lion."[9]

The Voyage of the Dawn Treader has the longest such passage. At the end of the voyage, they ask Aslan (in the shape of a lamb—a frequent symbol for Jesus in the Bible) whether they can enter his country, as they have just seen Reepicheep do. The Lamb replies that for them the way to Aslan's country is not from here but from their own world. This is a startlingly new idea to them, since up until now they have associated Aslan only with Narnia, so he explains: "There is a way into my country from all the worlds."[10]

The meaning of this becomes clear in *The Last Battle*, where as the children enter more deeply into Aslan's land, they see their parents in England, waving to them as if from a boat approaching the dock, and they realize that "all the real countries . . . are only spurs jutting out from the great mountains of Aslan."[11] Access to Aslan's land is available for anyone, in any world including our own, who desires it.

Aslan then tells the children that Lucy and Edmund can never return to Narnia, and Lucy sobs because she thinks that this means she and Edmund will never meet Aslan again. He reassures her: "But you shall meet me, dear one." Edmund queries how this can be, and Aslan replies:

---

7. Ibid., 93.

8. The capitalization of "He" is an old tradition for referring respectfully to God or Jesus.

9. C.S. Lewis, *The Last Battle* (London: The Bodley Head, 1956; Reprint, London: Collins, 1980), 173.

10. *The Voyage of the Dawn Treader*, 208-209.

11. *The Last Battle*, 172.

[T]here I have another name. You must learn to know me by that name. That was the very reason you were brought into Narnia, that by knowing me here for a little, you may know me better there.[12]

Here Lewis is seeking to open the door between Narnia and our own world which he himself had found. In the background of this exchange is Lewis' experience of joy, and his sense that behind that nameless feeling of desire was God, drawing Lewis gradually towards Christian faith over many years. His expectation is that once Lucy and Edmund are back in our world, they too will have experiences of joy, which will be Aslan's way of drawing them towards his world. In Lucy's case in particular, she is unlikely to make the mistake Lewis made about the meaning of joy, but will easily recognize its source.

In some ways, Lucy and Edmund at this point stand for all of us, so that Aslan's words to them are Lewis' words to us: that Aslan is trying to communicate with us, to draw us to believe in him and pursue him to his land. Our job is to listen to the flashes of joy, and to follow. And hopefully our experience of Narnia will enable us to recognize where those flashes come from, and move towards their Source.[13]

I suppose there are two kinds of readers of the Chronicles. There are those (like many of the children who wrote to Lewis) who know of Jesus in this world, bring their knowledge of him to the stories, and quickly recognize that Aslan is Jesus in a different form. And there are those who know little or nothing of Jesus in our world, but are drawn to the figure of Aslan in Narnia. If those in the first group take their knowledge of Jesus into Narnia and learn more about Jesus there, those in the second group bring their knowledge of Aslan into our world to learn more about him by his name in this world.

---

12. *The Voyage of the Dawn Treader,* 209.

13. Of course, unless one is Reepicheep, who bypasses death and goes directly into Aslan's land, the way there "lies across a river" which we have to cross at some point. But even this is not an obstacle for Aslan, who has already conquered death. So he can say, *"[D]o not fear that, for I am the great Bridge Builder" (*Voyage of the Dawn Treader,* 209).

Yet whichever direction the search flows, Lewis' intention is clear: that our knowledge of Aslan in Narnia should enrich our knowledge of Jesus in this world. Not that he is claiming information about Aslan that is not available in our world. As he wrote to a mother who was concerned that her son loved Aslan more than he loved Jesus: "the things he loves Aslan for doing and saying are simply the things Jesus did and said."[14] No: Lewis' concern is rather that our experience of Aslan in Narnia should give us a fresh understanding for who Jesus really was and is.

Does this mean, then, that the Narnia stories are simply an allegory, where one can say that a certain thing in the Chronicles "is really" or "represents" something in the biographies of Jesus? Lewis did write an allegory, *The Pilgrim's Regress*, in 1933, but he is very clear that Narnia is not a story of that kind. He wrote quite sternly to a class of fifth graders in Maryland that they should not think of everything in Narnia as "representing" something in this world. While *The Pilgrim's Progress* does that, he stresses, Narnia is of quite a different literary genre.[15]

Certainly there are parallels, as his letter to Hila indicates—otherwise those clues would have been meaningless. But there are also significant differences. For instance, Aslan dies for one person only (Edmund), whereas Christians believe Jesus died for the whole world. Or, again, Aslan takes different physical forms in different stories (a cat in *The Horse and His Boy*, an albatross and a lamb in *The Dawn Treader*), which Jesus never did.

So what does it mean that there are parallels but not exact ones? that Narnia has some marks of allegory but is not fully so? What kind of stories are these? Lewis' own answer was that the Chronicles are a "supposal." Suppose that the God of Christian faith had created another

---

14.   *Letters to Children*, 52. This child, Laurence Krieg, tells the story from his point-of-view, on the website <http://home.comcast.net/~krieg5208/Lewis/index.htm>.

15.   *Letters to Children*, 44. He is referring to *The Pilgrim's Progress* by John Bunyan (1628-1688).

world, different from ours, and that that world, like our own, had got into trouble and needed rescuing. What might that kind of a God choose to do about it?[16]

In fact, this is what all authors do who transpose a known character into a new situation. What, for example, will Anne of Green Gables be and do once she leaves Avonlea on Prince Edward Island and goes to teachers' college on the mainland? Author Lucy Maud Montgomery has to create a "supposal": Anne will be recognizably the same, so that some of her responses to new situations will be "typical" of the old Anne ("That's just what she did in a similar situation back home," we might say); whereas in other situations she will respond in a way that is still "her" but is new in our experience of her ("I guess that is what Anne would do under those circumstances"). This is the sort of thing Lewis is trying to do with the character of Jesus.

Why does Lewis bother? It is clear why an author like Montgomery needs to "suppose" what happens to her fictional character. But why does Lewis want to create Jesus in a different world? His motivation is quite different from hers, and connects with the story of his spiritual journey.

As a young person, he found himself thoroughly disillusioned with the religion he grew up with, finding it unimaginative and impossibly demanding. He called it "the dry husks of Christianity." By the time he reached Malvern College, where chapel attendance was mandatory, chapel meant "no more than two hours of blessed inactivity in which to dream his dreams secure from interruption."[17]

Lewis parodies this kind of religion in *The Pilgrim's Regress*. Early on, the Steward (who stands for the priest or pastor of a church: this is an

---

16.   Ibid., 92. A parallel kind of "supposal" happens in *Out of the Silent Planet* and *Perelandra*, two parts of *The Cosmic Trilogy* (London: Pan Books, 1990). The premise of *Perelandra*, for example, he explains like this: "Suppose, even now, in some other planet there were a couple undergoing the same temptation that Adam and Eve underwent here, but successfully" (*Letters of C. S. Lewis*, 475).

17.   Warren Hamilton Lewis, 232.

allegory, remember) takes a big card covered in small print down from a peg, and gives it to John, the hero (and Lewis' alter ego). John finds that it contains a long list of all the things the Landlord (God) requires of his tenants. John realizes as he reads that he already breaks many of them every day, and "could not imagine not doing." The Steward then warns John that the penalty for breaking any of these rules is to be shut up for ever in "a black hole full of snakes and scorpions as large as lobsters." But then he adds that, of course, the Landlord is "such a kind, good man, so very, very kind" that, naturally, John will not want to offend him anyway.[18]

Many people would echo Lewis' story of an oppressive childhood religion that they were glad to be rid of when they reached early adulthood. For Lewis, however, that all changed when he became a Christian as an adult. Far from being a return to the misery of his childhood faith, what he discovered was a quite different Christianity from the one he had left, one that brought meaning and stability, laughter and friendship, as well as intellectual and emotional satisfaction.

But how was he to convey the joy of his new faith? The stories of Jesus which he had known all his life had not changed: it was his understanding of them that had changed. How then to tell those old stories so that they would strike the reader with that same vivid freshness that Lewis experienced? For him, it was almost as though he had had to go away from Christianity to find spiritual reality elsewhere, and then to realize that what he had discovered was merely a signpost pointing him back to Christianity. As T. S. Eliot expressed it: "the end of all our exploring/Will be to arrive where we started/ And know the place for the first time."[19] Lewis says something similar:

---

18. *The Pilgrim's Regress* (1933; London: Collins Fount Paperbacks, 1977), 30.

19. T. S. Eliot, "Little Gidding," from *The Four Quartets* (London: Faber and Faber, 1986), 48. Lewis and Eliot knew each other, but though they had some spiritual things in common, did not particularly appreciate one another's writing (Wilson, 286-287).

Sometimes I can almost think that I was sent back to the false gods[,] there to acquire some capacity for worship against the day when the true God should recall me to himself.[20]

The answer was to create a similar kind of experience for us, his readers. Lewis' strategy was first to send us on a magical journey to discover a world ruled over by an attractive and non-religious Christ-figure. Then he gave hints to "those who have ears to hear" that the fulfillment of the story is to be found back in our world where Aslan is known by "another name." When writing about why he wrote "fairy stories," Lewis mused on what he had hoped the Narnia stories might accomplish for his readers:

[S]upposing that by casting all these things into an imaginary world, stripping them of their stained-glass and Sunday school associations, one could make them for the first time appear in their real potency? Could one not thus steal past those watchful dragons? I thought one could.[21]

The "watchful dragons" are those instincts that guard us against anything that smacks of traditional religiosity. They wake at the sound of anything "churchy" and breathe out fire to drive back any who dare to approach us with religious language or ideas. Lewis knew from personal experience of his boyhood religion how damaging religion can be, and why the dragons have been trained to react as they do. But he knows also that when we are defending ourselves against religion, we are also protecting ourselves against the life-giving spirituality he had found at the heart of the Christian religion. Hence his hope to "steal past" the dragons with stories that do not give off that unpleasant churchy odor but convey the "real potency" he had found. And hence Narnia.

---

20. *Surprised by Joy*, 65.

21. "Sometimes Fairy Stories May Say Best What's to be Said," in *Of This and Other Worlds*, 72.

Thus the strategy of making Jesus into a Lion is to help us see freshly something we thought we had seen before, but not very accurately. I suspect Lewis would be glad if we found ourselves saying by the end of the Chronicles, "But I never knew Jesus was like *that*." To which he might reply, "Exactly!" My friend Mark Harris told me that while he was reading the Chronicles to his children, "One night, after a particularly moving encounter between Lucy and Aslan, the girls insisted they wanted to say their prayers to Aslan that night. I could hardly refuse!" More than one child has asked if he might pray to Aslan rather than to Jesus. Wise parents say yes, at least for a time.

4

NARNIA, AWAKE!

In deciding how to describe a new world, Lewis was faced with choices, the same choices we face when we are figuring out our beliefs about life. He could, for example, have worked with the assumption that the universe just happened, that it is a random happening in a meaningless universe. There is no god, no mind behind everything, no guiding spirit overseeing the birth of the universe. Many people take that as a starting point of their Big Story. Or he could have assumed the pantheist version of the story, that "everything is divine, that God and nature are identical."[1] There is no specific act of creation in this version, because God's relationship with the world is not one of creator and creation.

In fact, Lewis wanted his new world to express a Christian world-view—the Story that tells how the world was created out of nothing by an omnipotent creator with design and purpose. This is an important choice, since everything else in our Story depends on where and how we begin.

Before he describes for us the creation of Narnia, however, he steps back to put it into a broader context, a context much wider than Narnia

---

1. Alister MacIntyre, "Pantheism," in *The Concise Encyclopedia of Western Philosophy and Philosophers*, ed. J.O. Urmson and Jonathan Ree (New York: Routledge, 1992), 227.

itself. In Lewis' view, the universe in which the land of Narnia is set is one where there are multiple worlds, including our own. All of these worlds are created, and exist in time with a beginning and an end. *The Magician's Nephew* gives us a hint of this multiplicity of worlds, as well as a picture of a beginning and an end, a dying world and a world being born.

Early on in the story, Digory and Polly put on magic rings, and are transported to the Wood between the Worlds, "a sort of in-between place"[2] between worlds. For them, it turns out to be first of all the way from this world to the world of Charn and back again. But in that Wood there were many other such pools—"there were dozens of others—a pool every few yards as far as [the eye] could reach"—each one presumably with "a world at the bottom" of it. [3] Later they will discover that Narnia is to be found at the bottom of one of these pools. This is Lewis' clue that there are dozens, perhaps an infinite number, of worlds in this universe.

The world of Charn, when the children reach it, turns out to be an old world, shortly to come to an end. The appearance of the sun tells us about Charn's age. It is low in the sky, much bigger than our sun, and to Digory it looked like "a sun near the end of its life, weary of looking down upon that world."[4] Although it means jumping ahead, it is interesting to contrast this (as Lewis does) with the appearance of the brand-new sun on the first day of Narnia, which naturally looks younger: "You could imagine that it laughed for joy as it came up."[5]

For Lewis, few things that have been created go on for ever. Worlds come and go. Civilizations and cultures last only for a time. Only people (and, in Narnia at least, animals) are "immortals" and last forever.[6] This is true even of the magical world of Narnia. In *The Magician's Nephew*

2.   C.S. Lewis, *The Magician's Nephew* (London: The Bodley Head, 1955; Reprint, Penguin Books, 1965), 36.

3.   Ibid., 31.

4.   Ibid., 58.

5.   *The Magician's Nephew*, 95.

6.   "The Weight of Glory" in *Screwtape Proposes a Toast*, 109.

we read about its birth: but Narnia too will grow up, become old, and die. When Narnia dies, once again the sun's appearance will be an indicator of what is happening. When that time comes, it is Digory and Polly who recognize what is happening, because they saw such a sun once before: the Narnian sun at its ending is "three times—twenty times—as big as it ought to be, and very dark red."[7] According to Lewis' own calculations, Narnia began in the year 1900 of our time, and lasted for a total of 2,555 years of Narnian time.[8]

But this is to jump ahead. Let us go back to the beginning of Narnia—a new world in a universe of worlds, some old, some new, some in between.

Narnia begins in nothingness. Digory and Polly have accidentally brought Jadis, the evil queen of Charn, back from Charn to London in their own world. To put a stop to the chaos she starts to cause there, they put on their magic rings and manage to return to the Wood between the Worlds. To their dismay, however, they bring not only Jadis but also Digory's Uncle Andrew, Frank (a London cab driver) and his horse. Still trying to escape from Jadis the Witch, Digory and Polly jump into another pool (chosen really by the horse, who had simply "stepped into it to have a drink") and find themselves in . . . nothing-ness—dark, silent and still.

This is our first, unlikely glimpse of Narnia. The Witch's comment on the empty blackness is that "This is an empty world. This is Nothing." And, says, Lewis, "it was uncommonly like Nothing."[9] This is part of the Christian worldview, that God created everything out of nothing. Nothing existed before God created it. We have creativity too, of course, but Lewis is emphatic that we only have the ability to create out of what has been given us: God alone can create out of nothing—*ex nihilo*.

---

7.   *The Last Battle*, 149.

8.   Walter Hooper, *Past Watchful Dragons: The Narnian Chronicles of C.S. Lewis* (New York: Collier Books, 1971), 41-44.

9.   This and the references that follow in this section are from pp. 91 to 106.

There is a strong streak of what is called "perspectivalism" in the Narnia stories—indeed, in all of Lewis—and it might be helpful to introduce it now. By this I mean that he has a clear understanding of how people see things differently according to what they bring to a situation—their history, their outlook on life, and their character. In an essay on "Miracles," for example, he says that, contrary to popular opinion, "[e]xperience by itself proves nothing." We will each interpret our experience differently and attempt to "prove" things from it, according to the preconceptions we bring to it.[10]

To put this another way, people may share the same experience, but how they understand that experience and how they feel about it will vary according to what Story they live by. This is important for understanding how the spirituality of Narnia works, and is an idea that will recur in several chapters.

Different perspectives are clear right from the beginning of this scene of the birth of Narnia. The travelers react differently to the Nothing they are in according to who they are. The Witch says, "My doom has come upon me." Uncle Andrew asks for "a drop of spirits." The cabby looks on the bright side ("if we're dead . . . well, you got to remember that worse things 'appen at sea") and leads them in singing a harvest hymn of thanksgiving. The children join in; Andrew and the Witch do not. They respond differently to what is happening because they bring differing experiences and beliefs to the scene.

Then the silence of the Nothing is broken by a sound, an ethereal singing, indescribable except to say that, for Digory, it was the most beautiful sound he had ever heard. Then something begins to happen. Stars appear and simultaneously the watchers hear new music of "cold, tingling, silvery voices." It seems as if the First Voice, "the deep one," has made the stars appear in response to its song, and given them their voice.

---

10. "Miracles," in *God in the Dock*, 25-26. Perhaps the clearest statement of this view is the Epilogue to *The Discarded Image* (Cambridge University Press, 1964), 216-223. I am indebted for this reference to Brian McLaren.

Lewis is here picking up an ancient tradition, going back to Pythago-ras and Plato,[11] and picked up by Milton and Shakespeare, that the stars make harmonious music as they move. Lorenzo in Shakespeare's *Merchant of Venice*, for example, says "There's not the smallest orb which thou behold'st / But in his motion like an angel sings."[12] What Lewis adds to this tradition is his conviction that, if the stars do make music, it is because they echo the nature of their Creator: they sing because he gives them his own gift of singing.

But there is more to these stars than the fact that they sing. Towards the end of *The Voyage of the Dawn Treader*, the travelers encounter Ramandu, a "retired star." He explains that, having reached the end of his life as a star, he was carried to this island. Here "a bird brings me a berry from the valleys in the Sun" every day, so that gradually he gets younger again. Finally he will become like a newborn child and rise to the skies to take his place in "the great dance" once again.[13]

Lewis is aware that this way of talking sounds fanciful to our ears. So when the practical Eustace, with his knowledge of science, says to Ramandu: "In our world . . . a star is a huge ball of flaming gas," Ramandu corrects him: "That is not what a star is but only what it is made of."[14] Lewis is gently drawing our attention to different ways of describing things. There is the scientific description, which in our culture we tend to endow with great authority, and which Eustace prefers. And there is (in this case) the poetic or imaginative description, which we tend to regard as inferior, or at least less real. But Ramandu, or Lewis through him, is reminding us that each kind of language has its own rightful sphere. It is not wrong to call stars balls of flaming

---

11. Circa 530 BCE and 427-347 BCE respectively.

12. *The Merchant of Venice*, V:I: 60-61.

13. *The Voyage of the Dawn Treader*, 176-177. In a later story, when Caspian worries that two stars might collide, Dr. Cornelius assures him: "The great lords of the upper sky know the steps of their dance too well for that" (*Prince Caspian* [London: Geoffrey Bles, 1951; Harmondsworth: Puffin Books, 1962], 49).

14. *The Voyage of the Dawn Treader*, 176-177.

gas—but it is rather limited. Even if a star is on one level a material object, the full reality of a star—its beauty and vibrancy, its mystery and poetry—requires other kinds of language. Thus for Lewis it is not naïve to call stars "showers of glittering people, all with long hair like burning silver and spears like white-hot metal."[15] Each description is trying to convey something different, but he would argue that the poetic brings home to us more of what a star really is.

The same is true for descriptions of other aspects of creation too. The scientific description has its uses, but it is one-dimensional, and Lewis wants us to feel much more than that—the richness and wonder of the world and its creation—through the way he describes it. Thus, as the voice continues to sing, things continue to spring into existence. In fact, different kinds of music seem to bring into being different kinds of thing: sun, grass, flowers, trees, animals—all are brought forth by changes in sound. As Polly observes, "When you listened to his song, you heard the things he was making up: when you looked round you, you saw them."[16] There is a deep empathy between whoever the creator is and the creation: it is as though each thing created represents something different in the character of the creator. As Lewis writes elsewhere, "Everything God has made has some likeness to Himself."[17]

Each new creation comes into being with joy, its colors "fresh, hot, vivid," responding gladly to the song of the creator. There are some worldviews, some versions of the Story—even some versions of the Christian Story—which see the material world as a bad thing, or at least an unfortunate necessity which spiritually-minded people will do their best to avoid. Clearly Lewis does not share this view. God, he says, is a materialist who invented matter because he actually likes it. There is no

---

15.   *The Last Battle*, 143. One biographer says that for Lewis, "Stars were a living silver, bursting into flame in answer to an eternal music in the mind of God" (Wilson, 127).

16.   *The Magician's Nephew*, 99.

17.   C. S. Lewis, *Mere Christianity* (London: Geoffrey Bles, 1952; Reprint, London: Collins Fontana Books, 1977), 143.

sense in which the "spiritual" is superior to the "physical."[18] This is why Christianity is the most materialistic of the world's religions. Thus the creation of the physical world of Narnia brings great joy to the Creator, to the creatures—and to those observers whose view has not already been prejudiced.

Then for the first time they see the singer: a lion, "huge, shaggy and bright"—The Lion, Aslan. The whole of this new creation is apparently coming "out of the Lion's head." Again, the different reactions of the watchers are significant. Uncle Andrew wants to shoot the lion ("Garn!" said the Cabby. "You don't think you could shoot 'im, do you?"). The Witch, who "understood the music better than any of them," throws the iron bar she wrenched from the London street lamp at the lion's head. The horse whinnies as if entering a second childhood. Polly experiences "an unspeakable thrill." The cabby feels awe in the presence of a wonderful mystery ("I'd ha' been a better man all my life if I'd known there were things like this").

Here again are different perspectives. Because of who they are, the Witch and Andrew are repelled by what is happening. The Witch "felt that this whole world was filled with a Magic different from hers and stronger. She hated it." They both want to get out of there as quickly as possible. So instead of enjoying the moment (which they are incapable of doing), they try to steal the magic rings from the children. The Witch accuses Andrew of trying to escape without her. Andrew accuses her of having embarrassed him in polite London society, an unforgivable sin. Both are self-centered, thinking only of their own power and advantage: no wonder they clash with one another, and even more that they want to avoid the Lion, whose whole being seems to run counter to theirs.

Again it is the cabby who has the most appropriate reaction: "Watchin' and listenin' 's the thing at present; not talking." And he is right. In the presence of this kind of love and power and creativity, the best response is simply to stand still and experience it to the full. It is

---

18. Ibid., 62.

this kind of instinct in Frank which suits him for the role he is soon to play in the new world.

But before he is given that role, there is another piece to the creation of Narnia—indeed, the centerpiece, the creation of the inhabitants of Narnia. Here we will find clues as to how Lewis answers the question, Who are we?

5

ALL CREATURES
GREAT AND SMALL

In the movie *Schindler's List*, there is a poignant scene where Oskar Schindler is bartering with a Nazi officer, Goeth, trying to bribe him to release Jews to work in his factory rather than face the gas chambers. But how much is it appropriate for Schindler to pay for each one? How can you measure? "What is a person worth to you?" asks Goeth.

The question of the worth of persons is a worldview question, and an important one. After all, how we answer the question "Who are we?" will affect the way we treat people. I once heard atheist philosopher Kai Neilsen say, "Human beings are big-brained lumps of slime." That is one answer to the question. Speaking for myself, however, I cannot imagine why I would treat a big-brained lump of slime with a great deal of respect.

So how do we view people? As meaningless products of a random universe? As soft machines, slaves to our genetic inheritance? As objects for us to exploit and make use of? Or as waves on the surface of the ocean of the universe, here for only a moment? There are many possibilities, each part of a different Story.

For Lewis, the most important thing that can be said about people is that they are made in the image of God, and their dignity comes from the fact that in some ways they resemble the Creator who made them. In one sense, everything God makes bears some resemblance to the Creator—in the same way that everything an artist creates is marked by her style, almost as clearly as if she had signed it. But there is a sense in which human beings are uniquely like God—much as an artist's self-portrait resembles her in a unique way. This is reflected in the description of Narnia's beginning.

When the work of creation is finished, "the Lion was quite silent." Then, like Noah in a different world,[1] he calls two of every species to him. These are to be the Talking Animals, the leaders of this new world. He looks at them "as hard as if he were going to burn them up with his mere stare"[2] and then he breathes on them "a long, warm breath." Throughout the stories, the breath of Aslan signifies the spirit of Aslan coming upon people and animals, giving them courage and strength to do what they could not otherwise have done. (Almost certainly Lewis had in mind the fact that the Greek word *pneuma* means both breath and spirit.) This is the first, and perhaps the most dramatic, of these occurrences. Then the stars sing again, this time "a pure, cold, difficult music." There is a flash of fire. And Aslan speaks:

> Narnia, Narnia, Narnia, awake. Love. Speak. Be walking trees. Be talking beasts. Be divine waters.[3]

Gods and goddesses step out of the trees. Fauns and satyrs and dwarfs appear. Aslan has apparently created not only those animals and plants we regard as "natural" but also those we think of as "mythological." Such distinctions are not so easy to make in Narnia (or for that matter in Lewis' mind). Then they and the talking birds and animals Aslan has chosen all speak in response:

---

1. Genesis 7:9

2. *The Magician's Nephew*, 107. This is the same use of the word "mere" as in Lewis' *Mere Christianity*. The Oxford English Dictionary includes among the meanings of "mere": undiluted, pure, absolute, and perfect.

3. Ibid., 108.

"Hail, Aslan. We hear and obey. We are awake. We love. We think. We speak. We know."[4]

Now the parallels between the Creator and the creation are clear. Aslan speaks, loves, thinks, and knows; those creatures he chooses to be the leaders of life in Narnia can also speak, love, think and know. They are as like him as it is possible for mere creatures to be, representing him and his nature to their world. This they can do as long as they continue to "hear and obey."

There is another characteristic of Narnia which at first sight seems quite alien to our culture, but the way Lewis explains it makes a lot of sense. It is this: that in Lewis' world, there is always hierarchy; indeed, there has to be hierarchy. Not that he is anti-democratic, but he sees democracy as a concession to our self-centered human nature rather than an ideal: democracy is a necessary medicine for our present sickness because self-centered people will always abuse hierarchy. "Mankind is so fallen that no man can be trusted with unchecked power over his fellows." Democracy provides "protection against cruelty." [5]

Nevertheless, democracy is not the ideal, nor the way the universe is fundamentally constituted. He would argue that hierarchy is "intrinsically as good and beautiful as the nakedness of Adam and Eve,"[6] and both are possible only in an unspoiled world. As a result, in the world of Narnia before evil has any influence, we see something of Lewis' vision for how hierarchy can work in a way that is not oppressive but a celebration of difference, a reflection of the dance that energizes the universe.[7]

---

4. Ibid., 109.

5. "Equality," in *Present Concerns* (New York: Harcourt Brace Janovich, 1986), 17.

6. Ibid.

7. We see the same image in Lewis' portrayal of the unspoiled—and hierarchical—worlds of Mars (Malacandra) in *Out of the Silent Planet,* and Venus (Perelandra) in *Perelandra..*

Narnia has been created "out of the Lion's head" and inescapably reflects something of his character, and so it follows that the Creator should set the tone for how this world will function. That tone is one where there is hierarchy, but there is also love, and, the more power you have, the more you are expected to serve:

> "Creatures, I give you yourselves," said the strong, happy voice of Aslan. "I give to you forever this land of Narnia. I give you the woods, the fruits, the rivers. I give you the stars and I give you myself. The Dumb Beasts whom I have not chosen are yours also. Treat them gently and cherish them but do not go back to their ways lest you cease to be Talking Beasts. For out of them you were taken and into them you can return. Do not so."[8]

In three lines, Aslan speaks of giving no less than five times. The leaders receive Narnia from him as a gift in trust. Their attitude to the "Dumb Beasts"[9] represents how they are to treat the whole created order: they are given power in order to be responsible, to take care of the world. This is how the Creator is: this is how they are to be like him.

This responsibility also comes with an equal and opposite warning. Now they are Talking Beasts, they are to behave in a way becoming of their dignity. The balance of Narnia's ecosystem depends on each behaving like itself. It upsets the natural order when people and animals seek to be more than they are created to be,[10] on the one hand, or when they fall into behaving as less than they were made to be, on the other. Thus if the Talking Beasts deny their nature, they will lose their nature

---

8. *The Magician's Nephew*, 109.

9. The word "dumb" does not have the connotation of "stupid" which it almost invariably has in North American culture. Here it has its original and literal meaning, "voiceless" or "without speech."

10. In Tolkien's mythology, also, problems arise when creatures seek to be more than they were made to be. Melkor, the angel who leads rebellion against the Creator, "sought . . . to increase the power and glory of the part assigned to himself" (J.R.R. Tolkien, *The Silmarillion* [Allen and Unwin, 1977; HarperCollins, 1999], 16)..

as Talking Beasts. This is not an arbitrary punishment, but one built into the very structure of that world's reality.

In this world of Narnia, then, every being needs to know what it is created to be in the great chain of being.[11] Each one needs to be conscious of the unique way it reflects the Creator, and of its part in the dance of the universe, and to fulfill that calling with wholehearted passion. Later in this scene, the dwarves make crowns and Lewis comments, "how those dwarves loved their work!" It is what they were made to do and thus what they do well. Aslan also sets two moles to dig—"which was what they liked best." As Lewis writes elsewhere: "A mole must dig to the glory of God and a cock must crow."[12] This is what they do in Narnia, and it brings joy.

Aslan's creation of hierarchy is not finished yet, however. First, he appoints an inner council of seven creatures to consider what to do about the evil that has entered the world with the Witch. Then he appoints an unlikely king and queen of Narnia, Frank the cabby and his wife Helen.

Frank and Helen are very taken aback by the idea, not having had "much eddycation, you see."[13] Of course, "eddycation" as far as Lewis is concerned is not the most important qualification for leadership, and may in fact be a handicap. Lewis always had a deep respect for "ordinary" people,[14] and Frank has already shown something of his

---

11. This is an Aristotelian term: Lewis's idea of hierarchy derives in part from Aristotle.

12. "Learning in Wartime", in *Fernseeds and Elephants and Other Essays on Christianity* (London: Collins Fontana, 1975), 32-33.

13. *The Magician's Nephew*, 129.

14. See, for example, the article, "A Christian Gentleman" by his driver (Lewis never learned to drive), Clifford Morris, in *C. S. Lewis at the Breakfast Table and Other Reminiscences*, ed. James T. Como (New York: Harcourt Brace Jovanovich, 1992), 192-201, where he is described as "the best of friends, the finest of companions, and the most excellent of conversationalists." See also the character of Sarah Smith, in C.S. Lewis, *The Great Divorce* (London: Geoffrey Bles, 1946; Reprint, HarperCollins, 1977), 118-119.

worth. While they were still in London, for example, and the mob was talking of stoning the Witch, who had been whipping the horse into a frenzy, and had struck a policeman with the iron bar from the lamp post, we are told that Frank, "obviously the bravest as well as the kindest person present," was occupied with trying to calm Strawberry.[15]

This is not the first time Frank has gone out of his way to take care of his horse. As he reminds Strawberry, even when they had little money in this world, "you did get a taste of oats when I could afford 'em."[16] In Lewis' worldview, not only is courage commendable but so is care for animals. Concern for animals indicates a person who understands how to use the power they have been allotted in the hierarchy of life, and such a person is thus well suited to govern animals in Narnia. (Part of Uncle Andrew's villainy, as we shall see, is his cowardice and his irresponsible use of animals.)

But Frank also has a latent spiritual sense. This is seen not only in his instinctive reaction to sing a hymn in times of difficulty[17] but, more importantly, in his vague recognition of Aslan. Aslan says to him: "Son . . . I have known you long. Do you know me?" To which Frank replies: "I feel somehow, if I may make so free, as 'ow we've met before."[18] In chapter 8, I will suggest ways in which Frank might have had a sense of Aslan's presence in the background of his life. But now Frank meets that mysterious Someone face-to-face.

Then Helen is summoned to join her husband, and clearly they are a well-matched couple. She has "a kind, honest face" and is not afraid of manual work ("she wore an apron, and her sleeves were rolled up to the elbow"). In most of the stories, people enter Narnia with pain and even trauma (as Frank and the others did on this occasion), but Helen, like Lucy on her very first visit,[19] has no difficulty: she is "fetched . . . quickly,

---

15. *The Magician's Nephew*, 89.
16. Ibid., 114.
17. Ibid., 92.
18. Ibid., 127.
19. *The Lion, the Witch and the Wardrobe*, 13.

simply, and sweetly as a bird flies to its nest," which suggests a spirit in immediate harmony with Aslan.[20] Perhaps she has known Aslan, and been known by him, before this time, even more closely than has her husband.

Then, together, Frank and Helen have explained to them the responsibilities of a leader in Narnia. They are very simple: to "rule and name" the creatures of Narnia, to treat them justly and to protect them from their enemies. And, asks Aslan, "if there was war, would you be the first in the charge and the last in the retreat?"[21]

In a word, Frank and Helen are to be stewards of this new world: to look after it and its inhabitants on behalf of the creator, in a manner which reflects the character of that creator. This is a different model of power from the one often seen in our world, where it is a pretext for self-interest, accumulation of yet more power, and the manipulation of those less powerful. In fact, this other way of using power is a characteristic of the lives of the rich and famous in Calormen. But at least Narnia starts out on the right foot. The gift of power is to benefit those who are ruled, just as Aslan himself uses his power for others.

Even the fact that Frank is uncertain about the last of the responsibilities Aslan lists—"I'd try—that is, I 'ope I'd try—to do my bit" is in his favour. To be too sure of yourself is not a virtue in Narnia.[22] As Aslan comments, "Then . . . you will have done all that a King should do."

The fact that these monarchs are to be different from those in our world is indicated by the fact that their crowns are not ugly and heavy, but "light, delicate, beautifully shaped circlets that you could really wear and look nicer by wearing."[23] *The Magician's Nephew* was published in

---

20. *The Magician's Nephew*, 107.

21. *The Magician's Nephew*, 128-130.

22. Later in the history of Narnia, another king, Caspian, will be applauded for the same diffidence. When he confesses his inadequacy, Aslan responds: "Good . . . If you had felt yourself sufficient it would have been a proof that you were not" (*Prince Caspian*, 175).

23. *The Magician's Nephew*, 159.

1955, two years after the coronation of Queen Elizabeth II, an event Lewis found very moving. It is tempting to see his reflections on that event as the backdrop for the coronation of Frank and Helen. He wrote to an American friend of how the "huge, heavy crown" was pressed onto the queen's "small, young head" (Elizabeth was twenty-five years old), and reflected how this was in some ways "a symbol of the situation of *humanity* itself," given the responsibility of stewardship by the Creator, and yet feeling inadequate. He added, "One has missed the whole point unless one feels that we have all been crowned and that coronation is, somehow, if splendid, a tragic splendour."[24]

It is as though Lewis is saying that monarchy (and by extension all authority) in our world easily becomes ugly and heavy, like such crowns, bending the spirit of the wearer, and hence "a tragic splendour." In Narnia, on the other hand, monarchy and the exercise of power are still things of beauty, to be worn lightly, a calling that is actually becoming to the wearer.

Who are we? In the world of Narnia, all is created as an expression of the Creator's love, beauty and power. Those who receive the power of speech, whether human, animal or mythological, have a particular role to give leadership in Narnia, but there is neither pride among those who lead nor resentment among those who follow. There is also immense diversity among those created—everything from nymphs to elephants and from dwarfs to unicorns—each reflecting something special of the nature of Aslan. All have their beauty, all have their unique place in the great dance.

It is an ideal world that makes us yearn (as Lewis undoubtedly intends we should) for the innocent perfection of the Garden of Eden. But, like our own world, Narnia does not stay that way for long.

---

24. C.S. Lewis, *Letters to an American Lady* (Grand Rapids: Eerdmans, 1967; 1971), 18.

6

A NEEVIL IN THE WORLD: TREACHERY

Something is wrong in the world. I doubt whether there is any philosophy, religion or lifestyle that is based on the belief that the world is just fine as it is. Where Stories differ, of course, is on just what it is that is wrong with the world—and what can be done about it. The world of Narnia too has its problems, and the way Lewis portrays them reflects his convictions about the nature of the problems in our world. Because the first Narnian animals in *The Magician's Nephew* have no experience of evil, when they first hear Aslan say the word, they think he must be talking about another beast called "a neevil."[1] The correct word for Lewis' understanding of the problems of Narnia and of our world, however, would be "sin," a useful shorthand term for identifying a range of problems which have some characteristics in common.

Where sin and evil begin is a mystery in that world as in ours. In the Narnia stories, you could say that it starts with the coming of Jadis the White Witch into the world at its very creation. But of course this only pushes the problem back in time. Where did she come from, and how did she become evil herself? All we know of her origins is that she is

---

1. *The Magician's Nephew,* 111.

the last of a long line of the rulers of Charn, and that for some time each has been more evil than the last. As Digory and Polly view the statues of the rulers of Charn, they find that there is a progression from the earliest, who look "kind and wise," through those who "looked very strong and proud and happy, but they looked cruel"; to the most recent who were "still cruel but they no longer looked happy." At the end of this sequence sat Jadis, "with a look of such fierceness and pride that it took your breath away."[2] It seems then that, at least in Charn, evil grows over time (Lewis saw no evidence for the optimistic view that people grow better over time[3]): but still, the question of its origin is unclear.

The Last Battle also sheds some light on the question by introducing the figure of the evil god Tash. We are told little of this character, except that he has the body of a man, the head of a bird of prey, and four arms, each ending in five claw-like fingers. He is clearly a supernatural being, and inspires worship among the Calormenes. (Tirian recognizes him because he once saw a statue of Tash in a Calormene temple.[4]) In *The Last Battle*, Aslan explains to Emeth the Calormene that Tash will only accept service which is evil: for example, "if any man do a cruelty in my name, then . . . it is Tash whom he serves and by Tash his deed is accepted."[5] So there is a supernatural background to evil in Narnia, the power of Tash, who (presumably) initiates and encourages everything that is evil.[6]

If one wants to go a step further and ask, But where did Tash come from? the Chronicles give us no answer. They do not go so far as Lewis'

---

2.   *The Magician's Nephew*, 48.

3.   He quotes approvingly the words of Boethius (480-524), that "all perfect things are prior to all imperfect things" and adds that this view "was common ground to nearly all ancient and medieval thinkers" (*The Discarded Image*, 85).

4.   *The Last Battle*, 79-80.

5.   Ibid., 156.

6.   "There was never any question of tracing all evil to man; in fact, the New Testament has a good deal more to say about dark superhuman powers than about the fall of Adam" ("Evil and God" in *God in the Dock*, 23).

Christian faith, which suggests that Satan (on whom Tash seems to be based) was originally a good angel who became a rebel against God[7]—although that too begs the question. The Chronicles, rather like the Bible, are more interested in the practical issue of how evil is played out in the lives of individuals, and how it can be countered. Whatever the primeval origins of evil, we are promised by Aslan that there is a deeper magic, from before the dawn of time, which will defeat evil.[8] It is a magic that was there long before evil came on the scene, and it will be there when sin and evil and death are only a long-distant memory. That is as much as we can know—but I suspect Lewis would tell us it is enough to live by, and that is all we need.

In terms of wisdom to live by, then, Narnia is full of examples of what can go wrong in the human spirit—and how it can be dealt with. Let me offer four case studies. Two in this chapter highlight our failings in terms of relationships. In the next chapter, two more case studies will look at the relationship between human evil and pride.

Case study #1: Edmund

Although *The Lion, the Witch and the Wardrobe* is probably the most famous of the seven Narnia stories, in some ways it is the least sophisticated.[9] Its portrait of human evil, for example, is drawn in fairly broad, general strokes, and it is left to the later books to develop more spiritual subtlety and psychological insight. Nevertheless, there is one funda-

---

7.   In the same way, Melkor in Tolkien's *The Silmarillion* is an angel who became a rebel against the creator Iluvatar. Sauron in *The Lord of the Rings* is "but a servant" of this "Great Enemy," as Aragorn calls him. *The Fellowship of the Ring*, I:XI, 210.

8.   *The Lion, the Witch and the Wardrobe*, 148.

9.   "Tolkien said that . . . it seemed like a jumble of unrelated mythologies. Because Aslan, the fauns, the White Witch, Father Christmas, the nymphs, and Mr. and Mrs. Beaver had quite distinct mythological origins, Tolkien thought that it was a terrible mistake to put them together in Narnia, a single imaginative country" (*Jack*, 312).

mental point which *The Lion, the Witch and the Wardrobe* makes clear. Evil is not in the first place just a matter of wrong actions: it is primarily an attitude of the heart towards the Creator, an attitude which says "No" to God.

Peter, Susan, Edmund and Lucy are staying for the summer in an old house owned by an elderly and eccentric professor. There Lucy discovers that she can enter the magical world of Narnia through an old wardrobe. Shortly afterwards, Edmund follows her lead, but in Narnia he meets the White Witch, the illegitimate ruler of Narnia, who ensures that it is "always winter but never Christmas."[10] The Witch, who is aware of ancient prophecies foretelling her destruction at the hands of four human children, immediately begins to seduce Edmund into being her ally with simple temptations such as Turkish Delight. She knows, as Edmund does not, that the enchanted candy is addictive, and that it will finally kill the one who is addicted to it.[11]

There is little subtlety about her temptations. Having appealed to his greed, she then appeals quite transparently to his pride, "the pleasure of being above the rest."[12] She is looking (she says) for a boy whom she can make her heir and who will take over the ruling of Narnia after her death:

> While he was Prince he would wear a gold crown and eat Turkish
> Delight all day long; and you are much the cleverest and handsomest
> young man I've ever met.[13]

Without any resistance, Edmund begins to surrender. On one level, he surrenders to flattery and greed; yet there is a deeper question behind that, the question of loyalty: whose side is Edmund on? The answer becomes clear when he returns to this world and Lucy warns him that the White Witch is evil. For Edmund the wonderful memory of the

---

10.   *The Lion, the Witch and the Wardrobe*, 23.

11.   Ibid., 38.

12.   *Mere Christianity*, 197.

13.   *The Lion, the Witch and the Wardrobe*, 39.

candy overrules the danger signals: "[h]e was already more than half on the side of the Witch."[14]

To be on the side of the Witch, however, is to be on the side of evil and against good. Shortly afterwards, when all four children have entered Narnia, they hear for the first time about Aslan. What is revealing is how the mention of Aslan affects each child differently. For Peter, Susan and Lucy, the name conjures up images of intense yearning and joy. Edmund, however, "felt a sensation of mysterious horror."[15] It seems that each child already has an internal disposition either to be drawn to Aslan or to be repelled by him: the mention of the name brings to the surface something which was previously only implicit.[16] Edmund is the only one of the four who reacts negatively to the name. The reason is obvious: he has a different perspective because he has already turned away from Aslan and given his allegiance to the Witch—and it has affected him deeply. Mr. Beaver already had a hunch that this was the case. For him, after years of living in Narnia, Edmund "had the look of one who has been with the Witch and eaten her food."[17]

The shift in Edmund's spirit cannot be isolated: it affects even his face. What is important about Edmund's actions is not in the first place the specific things he has done wrong—that he has been greedy for Turkish Delight and wanted to be a prince in Narnia—but that he has become the servant of the White Witch. In effect, he has said "No" to Aslan, even before he is conscious that Aslan exists.

Who we give our ultimate loyalty to, however, affects every other loyalty and every other relationship. Whatever that commitment is acts like a powerful magnet that turns everything in its direction. Thus Edmund's turning away from Aslan means first of all that his relation-

---

14.   Ibid., 42.

15.   Ibid., 65.

16.   Lewis' understanding here is similar to that of John's Gospel, where people are moving either towards the light or away from the light, and those who love the light will welcome Jesus' coming, e.g. John 3:19-21.

17.   *The Lion, the Witch and the Wardrobe*, 80.

ships with other people become twisted and off-kilter. For instance, he finds himself distanced from the other children. He imagines that it is they who have changed, but in fact it is he who is different. Instead of being involved in the adventure, like the others, he is more concerned about himself and what the others think of him:

> He kept on thinking that the others were taking no notice of him and trying to give him the cold shoulder. They weren't, but he imagined it.[18]

This theme of self—what I think of myself and how others perceive me—is one that recurs throughout the books.

It is not only Edmund's relationship with other people which becomes dislocated, however. Because Narnia is primarily inhabited by talking animals, and since Aslan himself is an animal, the way visitors to Narnia treat animals tells us something about who they are. So, when Edmund comes across the statue of a lion whom the Witch has turned to stone, whereas the other children would have felt profound pity (as indeed they do later[19]), Edmund's response is one of scorn. He takes out a pencil and draws a moustache and a pair of glasses on the lion.[20] It is a trivial thing on one level, but it is an indication that something has gone wrong for Edmund: he has no sense of compassion.

Thus there is a trickle-down effect from his original change of loyalty. Following the Witch affects his relationships with other people and with animals. Elsewhere in the Chronicles, evil spreads even further and affects people's relationship with the environment, particularly with the trees. The Telmarines in *Prince Caspian*[21] and the Calormenes in *The Last Battle*[22] show their lack of loyalty to Aslan by cutting down good trees. Misplaced allegiance cannot be kept in isolation from the rest of life: everything is affected.

---

18. Ibid., 82.
19. Ibid., 153-156.
20. Ibid., 87.
21. *Prince Caspian*, 60.
22. *The Last Battle*, 21.

In some ways, the saddest thing about Edmund's defection is that it fails to bring him the satisfaction it promised. This, in fact, is another theme which surfaces from time to time in the Narnia stories: sin promises joy but fails to deliver it, while the converse holds true: Aslan frequently invites people to hardship, yet they find joy on the other side of trials. Thus when Edmund goes to tell the Witch that he has brought his siblings into Narnia, he expects that she will keep her promise to reward him. But she ignores him: she has simply used and exploited him, treating him with the same contempt with which he has treated the others, and now she has no further use for him:

> And when at last Edmund plucked up his courage to say, "Please, your Majesty, could I have some Turkish Delight? You—you—said—" she answered, "Silence, fool!"[23]

Sin, in this big sense of loyalty to anyone other than the Creator, lets us down and does not fulfill its promise—any more than the serpent fulfilled its promise to Adam and Eve.[24] As with the runaway son in Jesus' most famous parable,[25] however, Edmund's disillusionment acts as shock therapy which brings about the beginning of a change in him:

> All the things he had said to make himself believe that she was good and kind and that her side was really the right side sounded to him silly now.[26]

If the problems of Narnia were caused merely by doing wrong things, Edmund's restoration could have been brought about quite simply by his giving up Turkish Delight. The heart of the problem, however, is much deeper than that—his betrayal of Aslan—and so his redemption requires first of all a change in his relationship to Aslan.

---

23. *The Lion, the Witch and the Wardrobe*, 103.
24. Genesis 3:5.
25. Luke 15:11-24.
26. *The Lion, the Witch and the Wardrobe*, 105.

The Lion, the Witch and the Wardrobe, then, demonstrates that the problem of Narnia is not that people want too much candy, or that they want to be more important than others. For Lewis, such things are merely the symptoms of a much deeper problem, a disease of the heart. This is "sin"—an attitude of life, a mindset, a heartset if you like—which is opposed to the reign of Aslan in Aslan's world. The cure is to become a subject of the true king—but that is very costly, both for the rebel and for the king. For the rebel, it requires him to lay down his arms. For the king, it costs him his life. We will return to this in chapter eight.

Case study 2: Eustace

As *The Voyage of the Dawn Treader* begins, Edmund and Lucy have come to stay with their cousin Eustace for the summer. We learn quickly what kind of person Eustace is:

> Eustace Clarence liked animals, especially beetles, if they were dead and pinned on a card. He liked books if they were books of information and had pictures of grain elevators . . . [D]eep down inside him he liked bossing and bullying . . . [H]e knew that there are dozens of ways to give people a bad time if you are in your own home and they are only visitors.[27]

Eustace is clearly of a practical turn of mind. Books are there as sources of rather boring facts. Beetles are best when dead and as objects of study. School is about getting marks, not about learning: "though he didn't care much about any subject for its own sake, he cared a great deal about marks."[28]

Not only is he selfish and practical, but he also lacks imagination. When he hears Lucy and Edmund talking about Narnia, he assumes that they are making up their stories of Narnia because "he was far too stupid

---

27.   *The Voyage of the Dawn Treader*, 7.
28.   Ibvid., 27.

to make anything up himself."[29] There is hardly any worse criticism of anyone in Lewis' world than to say that they lack imagination. For Lewis, Eustace is clearly ripe to be taught a lesson.

Then the three children are magically whisked into the Narnian ocean, and thence onto the deck of the *Dawn Treader*, a Narnian ship sailing in search of seven lost lords. Naturally, Eustace hates it. For one thing, he "kept on boasting about liners and motor-boats and aeroplanes and submarines."[30] Boasting in Narnia, as in our world, implies a desire to be more important, or at least, better than anyone else. It is a sign of Eustace's lack of joy. Those who have joy are those who throw themselves wholeheartedly into being who they were made to be, and are too busy doing that to be boastful. Eustace is not at this point . . . yet.

After a severe storm, they arrive at an island where they can find fresh drinking water and repair the ship. Eustace, wanting to avoid anything resembling hard work, slips off into the hills by himself for a rest. He comes by chance on the cave of a dragon at the point of death. He takes shelter from a storm in the dragon's cave, now vacant, and finds it filled with treasure. This should not have surprised him, but, of course, his reading about drains and exports had not prepared him to deal with dragons. When he awakes, he discovers that the unthinkable has happened: he has been transformed into a dragon. We are what we think: Eustace has been thinking "greedy, dragonish thoughts,"[31] and his thoughts assume dragonish flesh.

It is a recurring theme in the Chronicles that sin reduces our humanity. Frequently, the wrong-doers in Narnia are called "beasts"

---

29. Ibid., 10. Some of Lewis' more cultural biases also emerge in his description of Eustace: his parents were "vegetarians, non-smokers and teetotalers and wore a special kind of underclothes" (7). Eustace believes that girls should be treated the same as boys (28). He is a Republican and has no patience for Caspian's supposed kingship (28). He is a pacifist, and goes to a school without corporal punishment (31).

30. Ibid., 27.

31. Ibid., 73.

or "beastly."[32] Certainly this was a common term of reproach in the England of Lewis' time, yet it takes on a darker significance in this context. There is something about sin—being out of harmony with our Creator—which has a tendency to make us less than we are meant to be, even less human. Sin may tempt us to try and become more than we were made to be, but its effect is ultimately to make us less than we were made to be.[33]

C. S. Lewis has a deep conviction that our choices make us who we are. If we make selfish choices, we will become selfish people. If we make generous choices, we become generous people. In the words he puts in the mouth of George MacDonald, if we choose to grumble, at first:

> Ye can repent and come out of it again. But there may come a day when you can do that no longer. Then there will be no *you* left to criticise the mood, nor even to enjoy it, but just the grumble itself going on forever like a machine.[34]

In the case of Eustace, the self that he has chosen to become—selfish, boastful, lazy—has taken on a vivid outward expression, a metaphor for the state of his heart: he is a dragon outwardly as well as inwardly.

For Edmund, the shock of not receiving what he had been promised had been a turning point. For Eustace, it is the horror of finding himself a dragon which begins a change in him, and to that extent his transformation is a good thing. He discovers that he wants to be with other people, to "talk and laugh and share things." He is a lonely monster. The realiza-

---

32.   The references are too numerous to list. For example, in the *The Lion, the Witch and the Wardrobe*, Peter says to Edmund, "You've always liked being beastly to anyone smaller than yourself" (45); later he says of Edmund, "Well, of all the poisonous little beasts . . ." (55). In *The Magician's Nephew*, Digory says of his uncle, "You are a beast" (28); and, on hearing of Jadis' callousness, Polly mutters, "Beast!" (66).

33.   In a parallel way, the mulish Rabadash in *The Horse and His Boy* will be turned into a donkey (C. S. Lewis, *The Horse and His Boy* [London: Geoffrey Bles, 1954; Reprint, Harmondsworth: Puffin Books, 1965]).

34.   *The Great Divorce*, 69.

tion dawns that it is he who has been at fault, not his friends. "He longed for their voices."[35]

If evil drives people apart into isolation, one sign of redemption is that they want to come together again. Up to now, Eustace has perceived himself as apart, even aloof, from the community: now he longs to be a part of it. The others want to receive him back into the community, but cannot decide what they will do with him in his dragon form when they are ready to set sail. For Eustace, this comes to symbolize what a misfit he had chosen to be before: since the day he boarded the *Dawn Treader*, he had been "an unmitigated nuisance and . . . he was now a greater nuisance still."[36]

This is not the end of Eustace's lesson, however. It is one thing to realize how we have gone wrong, but it is quite another to be able to change. And this Eustace cannot bring about for himself. Before we turn to the question of "What is the solution?" however, there is more to be said about the problem. Things will get worse before they get better.

---

35. *The Voyage of the Dawn Treader*, 74.
36. Ibid., 83.

7

THE HEART OF THE
MATTER: PRIDE

In Christian tradition, pride has the reputation of being the worst of sins.[1] In *Mere Christianity*, Lewis says that, compared with pride, other sins are "mere fleabites." Pride is "the essential vice, the utmost evil. . . . it is the complete anti-God state of mind."[2] Maybe Lewis wrote this strongly because he recognized it as his own "besetting sin," and struggled with it for years.[3] Ultimately, pride is the desire of human beings to put themselves in the place of God. When it is translated into the context of human relationships, pride becomes the desire to make ourselves more important than we really are, inevitably at the expense of others.

We saw something of the beginnings of this tendency in Edmund and Eustace, with their misplaced allegiances and soured relation-

---

1. "Augustine, Aquinas and Dante all characterized pride as the ultimate sin, while Milton and Goethe dramatized it" (D. H. Tongue, "Pride" in *The New Bible Dictionary* [London: Inter-Varsity Fellowship, 1962]).

2. *Mere Christianity*, 106.

3. "[A]s he had told Arthur [Greeves], pride was his besetting sin" (Bremer, in Schulz and West, 53).

ships, but full-blown pride, its character and its dangers, are more fully explored in two of the other Narnia books, *The Horse and his Boy* and *The Magician's Nephew*.

Case study #3: Bree and Aravis

When *The Horse and His Boy* opens, we meet Shasta, the adopted son of a poor fisherman. One day a proud and powerful knight or Tarkaan stays at his house, and that night Shasta overhears the Tarkaan and the fisherman haggling over the price for which he might be sold into slavery. He discovers that the Tarkaan's horse, Bree, is a talking horse—a thing unknown in the country of Calormen though common enough in Narnia, the land to the north. They decide to escape together to Narnia and freedom. On the way, hunting lions force them to link up with another talking horse, Hwin, and her rider, a young and proud Tarkheena named Aravis. The book then tells of their adventures on the way to Narnia.

Through living in Calormen, "hiding my true nature and pretending to be dumb and witless like their horses,"[4] Bree has become proud. Like most proud people, one result of his pride is that he is worried about how he appears to others, and the thought of returning to Narnia, where he will not be familiar with the protocol, worries him. What about rolling on his back, for example, which he loves? Maybe horses in Narnia do not do it; maybe it is "a silly clownish trick" he has picked up from "ordinary" horses. Perhaps, without knowing it, he has acquired a lot of "low, bad habits" in Calormen, and will appear foolish in the sophisticated society of Narnia.[5]

Or again, when the group have to pass through the enemy city of Tashbaan, the horses have to be made to look like work horses, rather than the war horses they really are. Hwin is merely practical about the matter (one of the few times in Narnia that being practical is a virtue), but:

---

4.   *The Horse and his Boy*, 18.

5.   Ibid., 26.

"My dear madam," said Bree. "Have you pictured to yourself how very disagreeable it would be to arrive in Narnia in that condition?"

"Well," said Hwin humbly (she was a very sensible mare), "the main thing is to get there."[6]

This is a very revealing exchange. For Bree, to arrive looking bedraggled would be "disagreeable." What he really means is that he would give a bad first impression, whereas he wants to be seen for the fine stallion he believes he is.[7] Hwin, on the other hand, speaks "humbly" because she is "sensible": for Lewis, to be humble is to be sensible, about who you are and who you are not.

Aravis also suffers from pride. She has grown up in a culture where she has always been treated as more important than others. As a result, when she makes her escape from her father's house, she thinks nothing of drugging her maid, even though she knows the consequences. When Shasta asks what happened to the maid, Aravis replies coolly that she was probably beaten for oversleeping. She adds casually that the maid was a spy of her stepmother's, and she was therefore "very glad they should beat her."[8] She obviously regards the maid as an inferior class of creature, and cares nothing for the injustice she caused to be done to another, as long as it serves her own purposes. In other words, she is a snob. Throughout the Narnia stories, it is a sign of being on the Lion's side to treat all creatures with respect, and a form of sin not to do so.[9]

---

6. Ibid., 46. In general, Lewis thinks the male of the species more conceited than the female. In *The Magician's Nephew*, he points out that Digory was always much more worried than Polly about looking foolish (162).

7. Elsewhere Lewis comments that this is not the worst kind of pride. "It shows that you are not yet completely contented with your own admiration. You value other people enough to want them to look at you. You are, in fact, still human." *Mere Christianity*, 110.

8. *The Horse and His Boy*, 42.

9. Lewis wrote about his hatred of snobbery in his essay "The Inner Ring," in *Screwtape Proposes a Toast*.

The climax of the story comes as they approach Narnia, just ahead of an attacking Calormene army headed by Prince Rabadash. A lion pursues them and leaps at Aravis. Shasta jumps from Bree's back to help in whatever way he can, but Bree continues to gallop for safety. Shasta manages to drive the lion back and they all reach safety. But the experience has been a revelation (literally: it has revealed things they did not know before) for each of them, particularly for Aravis and Bree. Bree, in particular, realizes that he is not the brave war horse he has believed himself to be up to this point. In spite of his track record of fighting in a hundred battles, now he has been "beaten by a little human boy—a child, a mere foal"—and he is totally humiliated.[10] Once again, it takes a crisis for the characters to realize their mistakes. For Bree, it is the fact that he is confronted publicly with his own failure and weakness.

At first, he finds the truth devastating—"I've lost everything," he wails. The hermit of the Southern March with whom they take refuge is a wise man, and he sees rather more deeply into Bree's problem. Bree has actually lost nothing but his unrealistically high opinion of himself. If he really has felt humility for the first time, this is a great opportunity to get to know himself at last—beginning with the realization that his time in Calormen had made him feel more special than he really is.[11]

For Lewis, there is a clear connection between humility and truth. If pride is thinking you are more than you really are, humility is not seeing yourself as less than you really are—but seeing yourself as your Creator sees you. Pride is a lie about yourself, humility the truth. Thus Aslan knows on the one hand that Bree is not the great horse he thinks he is, but on the other hand Aslan knows also that Bree is a "very decent sort of Horse" and that is all Bree is called to be. When he realizes that truth, he will know joy.

If *The Horse and his Boy* shows how there is hope of redemption from pride, *The Magician's Nephew* is darker and not quite so optimistic. If

10.   *The Horse and his Boy*, 128.
11.   Ibid., 129.

pride is "the complete anti-God state of mind," this book shows how dangerous it is.

Case study #4: Uncle Andrew

I have suggested that many of the problems of Narnia can be traced to failing to give Aslan our allegiance. The question then arises, however: Why should we give our allegiance to Aslan, or indeed to anyone but ourselves? After all, our society says things like:

"Be your own person."

"You decide what is true."

"Believe whatever you like."

"You choose what is right and wrong for you."

"Don't let anyone boss you around."

The whole concept of obeying a higher authority has never been popular, I suppose, but it has been particularly unacceptable in the West since the 1960s. This theme of "who's the boss?" is a useful question to bear in mind when reading *The Magician's Nephew*, especially in considering the portrait of Uncle Andrew.

The only reason that anyone from our world is present to witness the birth of Narnia is because of Digory's Uncle Andrew. For years, he has been involved in a "great experiment"[12] in magical travel. As the story opens, Digory and his friend Polly accidentally discover what Uncle Andrew is doing. Seizing the opportunity, Andrew tricks Polly into furthering his experiment: he gives her the gift of an attractive yellow ring, which she puts on—whereupon she disappears into another world. As Andrew guesses will happen, Digory feels he has no option but to follow her and try to bring her back.

Uncle Andrew is an interesting creation. C.S. Lewis creates him in such a way that much of his outlook on life sounds perfectly normal and right to our ears. For example, he is involved in an important experiment: we understand that experiments are necessary. He believes

---

12. *The Magician's Nephew*, 19.

he can decide for himself what is right and wrong: many would agree. He likes to make his own decisions: that is fundamental to Western democracies. He is practical: nobody wants to be accused of being impractical. He is willing to make sacrifices for greater ends: we admire people like that. All these things sound perfectly reasonable.

Yet as the story unfolds, it becomes clear that Uncle Andrew's outlook on life is totally inadequate. His experiment and his desire for power mean that everything else in his world becomes secondary, whether relationships or beauty, honor or goodness. His experiment causes him to behave callously towards both people and animals. His vision of the world, which really centers on himself, means that he is unable to acknowledge anything greater than himself. As Lewis puts it elsewhere, "as long as you are looking down, you cannot see something that is above."[13]

Andrew gives himself away when explaining to Digory what is involved in being a magician. He sees himself as possessing "hidden wisdom," and being "freed from the common rules."[14] Not surprisingly, his words sound remarkably like those of Queen Jadis, who also believes herself to be too great a queen to be bound by the rules that govern "common people." She too "must be free from all rules." Digory finds the words more convincing coming from her than from his uncle, however, since she is seven feet tall and dazzlingly beautiful.[15]

Like her, Andrew has a sense of belonging to an elite, an "inner ring", and of having access to knowledge that no-one else has. He believes that rules, at least the "common" rules, do not apply to him. He explains that he learned his art from his fairy godmother, as he also learned "to dislike ordinary, ignorant people."[16] In other words, he has forgotten that he too is an "ordinary," "common" human being like other ordinary,

---

13. *Mere Christianity*, 109.
14. *The Magician's Nephew*, 23.
15. Ibid., 61.
16. Ibid., 22.

common human beings. Once again, Lewis' hatred of snobbery is in the background.

Nor should we be too impressed by the fact that Andrew says he is also willing to give up "common pleasures": that can be just as perverse as trying to be free of responsibilities. Both imply pride and independence, and a rejection of God's good gifts.[17] For Lewis, who sees God as "a hedonist at heart,"[18] to reject pleasure, just as much as rejecting God's laws, can mean rejecting God. At first Digory is impressed with Andrew's self-sacrifice, particularly since he "looked so grave and noble and mysterious." But then Digory sees through the deception, and thinks to himself: "All it means . . . is that he thinks he can do anything he likes to get anything he wants."[19]

Digory is right. Fine words about freedom and sacrifice and a high calling cannot disguise the fact that, for Andrew, he is still the center of his own life.[20] Though many of his attitudes may sound "normal," in fact they are the expression of a mindset we have already met in *The Lion, the Witch and the Wardrobe*, an attitude of independence from the Creator. In a word, Andrew is a sinner.

As with Edmund in *The Lion, the Witch and the Wardrobe*, the characters' attitude to animals provides a touchstone which reveals their heart. Some of Andrew's experiments in time travel have involved attaching magic rings to guinea pigs. Some of them died, while others exploded "like little bombs." Digory, remembering a guinea pig of his own, reacts with the compassion Lewis' good characters always have for animals: "It was a jolly cruel thing to do." For Andrew, however, the

---

17. The New Testament may have such people in mind when it warns against some who "forbid marriage and demand abstinence from certain foods, which God created to be received with thanksgiving" (1 Timothy 4:3).

18. *The Screwtape Letters*, 127.

19. *The Magician's Nephew*, 24-25.

20. A similar character is the scientist Weston, in *Out of the Silent Planet*, who proclaims with similar self-centered motives, "Life is greater than any system of morality" (*The Cosmic Trilogy*, 121).

suffering of animals is irrelevant: his experiments are far more important. And in an important aside, he adds: "That's what the creatures were there for. I'd bought them myself." For Andrew, ownership has taken the place of stewardship (which is the right use of power in Narnia) and purchase is the true symbol of ownership. The guinea pigs are his because he bought them. He has forgotten that they were the Creator's before they were ever his, and that he has no ultimate rights to them. When Digory protests, Andrew explains:

> "You don't understand. I am the great scholar, the magician, the adept, who is doing the experiment. Of course I need subjects to do it on."[21]

We often say more than we mean. In this context, I cannot help wondering whether it is not significant that Uncle Andrew calls himself "I am," the ancient Hebrew name for God.[22] He also uses the word "subjects," primarily in a scientific sense—but, of course, the word also has a political sense: Andrew has made himself their sovereign, and they are his subjects. The problem with failing to give allegiance to Aslan is that we immediately come to think that we are more important than we really are—indeed, to think of ourselves as God in some sense. This, after all, was the essence of the very first temptation in Eden: "you will be like God."[23] Human beings can be very good at being human beings, but they are not created to bear the weight of being God.[24]

In *The Lion, the Witch and the Wardrobe*, it was hearing the name of Aslan which revealed what was in each of the four children's hearts. Now, in the same way, it is the coming of Aslan which shows up the hollowness of Uncle Andrew. His world has been entirely constructed around himself. He has been the supreme being in his own little universe. So when Aslan

---

21. *The Magician's Nephew*, 26-27.
22. Exodus 3:14.
23. Genesis 3:5.
24. Some consciously try. "Each soul is its own God. You must never worship anyone or anything other than self. For you are God. To love self is to love God" (Shirley Maclaine, *Dancing in the Light* [Toronto: Bantam Books, 1986], 343).

appears, singing into being a new world of color and beauty and vitality, the children love it, but Andrew hates it. They listen open-mouthed and with their eyes shining. But Andrew's "shoulders were stooped and his knees shook. He was not liking the Voice."[25] The coming of Aslan, after all, challenges the reality of everything Andrew has built his life on. Aslan embodies a different vision of power, one that is unselfish and loving. Even more, Andrew knows, somewhere deep down, that he has tried to usurp Aslan's role in his world. All this means that Aslan's appearance is deeply threatening.

Or consider the fact that Andrew's view of the newborn Narnia is practical and utilitarian. To be "practical" in Narnia is not particularly a compliment. Witches, for example, are only interested in things and people if they can make use of them for their own purposes: "they are terribly practical."[26] Among other dangers, being practical in Narnia means that you miss the point of what is really happening: you are looking down instead of up. So it is here. For Andrew, Narnia is an object, capable of making him rich and powerful if he exploits it wisely: "the commercial possibilities of this country are unbounded." He compares his "discovery" of Narnia to Columbus' discovery of America—though in this case a gun with which to shoot "that brute" would help to begin the conquest of this new world. And, what's more, "There's no telling how long I might live if I lived here."[27]

Aslan, on the other hand, has a totally different outlook. His first speech to the animals is all about giving; Uncle Andrew thinks only of getting. Aslan speaks of caring for those weaker than oneself; Uncle

---

25. *The Magician's Nephew*, 94-95.

26. Ibid., 71. Eustace, you will remember, was also of a practical turn of mind, and cared nothing for fantasy or adventure. Similarly, Arsheesh the fisherman was not interested in the North because "[h]e had a very practical mind" (*The Horse and His Boy*, 12).

27. *The Magician's Nephew*, 103. Columbus was still a hero in Lewis' time: the dark side of his discovery of America which we have learned since adds a darker irony to Andrew's boast.

Andrew sees the weak as serving the interests of the powerful. Aslan speaks of cherishing; Uncle Andrew speaks of using. Aslan warns of the danger of becoming less than one is created to be; Andrew wants to be more than he was created to be.

What is Andrew to do? In order to maintain the self-centered world he has constructed, and to resist the new spirit of love and self-giving which derives from Aslan, he is driven to desperate measures. He has to find a way to deny this new reality Aslan is creating. He needs a way to understand it and live in it which allows him to maintain his self-centeredness. As a result, he finds himself forced to distort the reality of what he is experiencing. Although Aslan is singing, Andrew tries to convince himself that it is really only roaring. It is a theme in Lewis' writing that God gives us what we choose, and as a result "the trouble about trying to make yourself stupider than you really are is that you very often succeed." Soon, Uncle Andrew succeeded: he really could hear only roaring. And, even more sobering, his choice in this direction limits his ability to choose anything else: "Soon he couldn't have heard anything else even if he had wanted to."[28]

As Lewis comments:

> what you see and hear depends a good deal on where you are standing: it also depends on what sort of person you are.[29]

Here again is Lewis' perspectivalism. All of us create our own interpretations of the world. God has given us the freedom and responsibility to do that. Yet, at the same time, we want as far as possible to be true to the world "out there" as we perceive it, and to be upfront about our limitations and our biases.[30] This is what Lewis means when he says our view of the world depends on "where you are standing" and "what sort

---

28. *The Magician's Nephew*, 117.

29. Ibid., 116.

30. Richard Middleton and Brian Walsh write about the difficulties of doing this in *Truth is Stranger than it Used to be: Biblical Faith in a Postmodern Age* (Downers Grove: InterVarsity Press, 1995), 31-33, 166-171.

of person you are." Andrew is a self-centered, power-hungry person, and therefore his perception of the world of Narnia is twisted by that internal bias. Sin always warps our perception of truth.

As a result, Andrew continues to disbelieve what is happening around him. He finds himself terrified of the newly-created Talking Animals, and becomes a figure of fun as they try to work out whether he is animal, vegetable or mineral. Polly asks Aslan to do something to rescue him from the humiliation, but of course Andrew has put himself into a position where, even if Aslan did try to speak to him, he would simply hear growling and roaring, and so he cannot be comforted.[31] Aslan gives him "the only gift he is still able to receive"—the gift of sleep—and Andrew is returned to our world.

What we see in Uncle Andrew, as with Edmund and Eustace, is the danger of not being a subject of King Aslan: yet here it is more fully spelled out. Because of the dangerous power human beings have, that of being able to choose, we can make ourselves unable to see or hear Aslan, so that we cannot receive his truth and his love. This is the state into which Andrew gets himself.

Aslan's comment on seeing Andrew's sorry state is telling: "[H]ow cleverly you defend yourselves against all that might do you good."[32] Aslan wants Uncle Andrew to experience joy, the kind of joy he could have if he will give up his self-centeredness and open his mind to the reality of Aslan. The children and other visitors to Narnia find such joy, but Andrew's ego is strong enough to defend him against such a disturbing gift. And Aslan will not force him to give in.

Thus Uncle Andrew is never redeemed through a face-to-face encounter with Aslan in the clear-cut way that Aravis and Bree, Edmund and Eustace, experience. But Lewis has not given up hope for him. At the end of the book, we are told that Andrew, having learned his lesson, gave up his magic and "became a nicer and less selfish old

---

31. *The Magician's Nephew*, 158.
32. Ibid., 158.

man" than he had been before.[33] The fact that he has given up magic suggests he has abandoned his self-destructive taste for power. And he has become "less selfish," which suggests he recognizes the existence and rights of others in the world, and thus a lessening of the pride which put him at the center of his own universe and threatened to destroy him.

These four portraits of the "neevil in the world" create a depressing impression. Lewis obviously has a bleak opinion (some might say simply a realistic opinion) of what human nature can do when left to its own devices. But in his view of the world, human beings are not left to their own devices—at least, not indefinitely. There is a Creator who cares about the trouble the creation gets into, and chooses to do something about it. That will be the subject of the next chapter.

---

33. Ibid., 171.

8

A DEEPER MAGIC

What is to be done about the troubles of Narnia? They seem beyond the resourcefulness of the wisest of kings. Only Aslan himself can save Narnia. He knows this right at the beginning of the stories, when Narnia is created and the Witch has already entered. He tells Digory, "Evil will come of that evil, but it is a long way off, and I will see to it that the worst falls upon myself."[1] But exactly how will he deal with evil, and what can he mean by saying that the worst will fall on him?

The death of Aslan

There is a little-known spiritual secret in Narnia, and it is this: there is great strength to be found in weakness.[2] The supreme example of this is in the death of Aslan. His willingness to deliver himself into the Witch's hand, to be bound, shaved, muzzled, humiliated and killed by the Witch and her army seems like the height of folly. The Witch herself certainly does not understand it: "The fool!" she cried. "The

---

1. *The Magician's Nephew*, 126.
2. This is also a driving principle in *The Lord of the Rings*.

fool has come. Bind him fast."[3] At this point, Lucy and Susan have not been with Aslan long enough to understand that he might choose this route: they hold their breath, waiting for Aslan to flex his muscles and scatter his enemies. But, of course, it never happens. His enemies cheer at their own imagined bravery, though, of course, the only reason they have power over him is that he allows them to. And the Witch thinks she has won. As she deduces, Aslan may die in place of Edmund, but, once he is out of the way, she can kill Edmund anyway, and all of Narnia will be hers without a rival. It looks like a *fait accompli.* What can go wrong?

What can go wrong is that weakness is not always weak, and the kind of strength the Witch wields is not always very strong. The Witch has appealed to the Deep Magic of justice, whereby "every traitor belongs to me as my lawful prey and that for every treachery I have a right to a kill."[4] This is the ancient principle that "the wages of sin is death," and it is so deep in the reality of Narnia that it is even "engraved on the scepter of the Emperor-beyond-the-Sea." Nothing can change it, and woe to those who suggest it. This is a strong kind of justice: an eye for an eye and a tooth for a tooth. If someone is guilty of betraying the lives of others, their own life is forfeit. There is a relentless logic to it.

But behind and above and before the principle of justice is a different principle: the principle of redemption. Justice is good, but redemption is better. Justice looks strong but may turn out to be weak. Redemption looks weak but turns out to be strong. The Witch understands justice but redemption is inconceivable to her.[5] For her, strength is strength is strength. Her interest is only in herself and in what will further her own kingdom. Others are there only to be used to further her cause. As a result, it never occurs to her that someone might be more concerned

---

3.   *The Lion, the Witch and the Wardrobe,* 138.

4.   Ibid., 128.

5.   The poet W. H. Auden wrote that evil "has every advantage but one—it is inferior in imagination. Good can imagine the possibility of becoming evil . . . but evil, defiantly chosen, can no longer imagine anything but itself" (cited by T. Shippey, *The Road to Middle Earth* [London: Allen and Unwin, 1985], 131).

for others than for himself, that someone might be willing to sacrifice himself for others. The thought would never enter her head. Her strength is hatred: love is Aslan's secret weapon. Thus she does not know the Deeper Magic that:

> ... when a willing victim who had committed no treachery was killed in a traitor's stead, the Table would crack and Death itself would start working backwards.[6]

So the lawful price for Edmund's treachery is paid as justice required—yet Aslan is alive again. His choice of weakness, the weakness of death, flowers into the strength of new life, for Edmund and for all of Narnia.[7]

Aslan calls people

If it is true that in order to enjoy Narnia fully, one has to know the creator of Narnia, how does one get to know Aslan? One answer is that he does not wait for us to start searching for him: he goes looking for us. There are times, for instance, when people think they have been looking for Aslan, but they find they are wrong. After Jill and Eustace have entered Narnia in *The Silver Chair*, Jill is surprised when Aslan speaks of having summoned them there. As far as she knew, all that happened was that she and Eustace, trying to hide from the school bullies, called out to Somebody with a name she had not heard before, hoping that the Somebody would help. Then they found the door open to a different world. But Aslan explains that there was another dynamic at work:

---

6.   Ibid., 148.

7.   Although in a direct sense Aslan dies only for Edmund, "if Edmund had been lost, the prophecy about the four thrones could not have been fulfilled and the White Witch would have ruled forever" (Michael Ward, "Lewis' Depictions of Conversion" in *C. S Lewis: Lightbearer in the Shadowlands: The Evangelistic Visions of C. S. Lewis*, ed. Angus J.L. Menuge [Wheaton: Crossway Books, 1997], 161).

"You would not have called to me unless I had been calling to you," said Aslan.

"Then you are Somebody, Sir?" said Jill.

"I am."[8]

Yet it is not always just a matter of Aslan calling on one specific occasion. Aslan's interest in people is more pervasive and long-lasting than that. When Frank the London cabby first meets Aslan, Aslan calls him "Son" and says, "I have known you long. Do you know me?" Frank is puzzled:

"Well, no, sir," said the Cabby. "Leastways, not in an ordinary manner of speaking. Yet I feel somehow, if I may make so free, as 'ow we've met before."[9]

Who is right? Has Frank known Aslan or not? Where had Frank "met" Aslan? Where indeed had Aslan "known" Frank? The answer is that Frank has known Aslan in a way. Things have happened in Frank's life where he sensed the presence of Aslan but did not know what it was nor what its name was. Aslan has known Frank, has perhaps protected Frank from dangers he was not aware of, perhaps blessed Frank beyond what he felt he deserved (maybe with his marriage to Helen, for example), given him strength on those freezing winter nights when he had to drive his cab.

Perhaps too Frank had sensed Aslan's reality in church—since Frank knows a hymn and used to sing in a church choir[10]—where Aslan would have been known by his other name. Or perhaps (as happens for many people), it was simply in the beauties, the questionings, and the difficulties of everyday life. So far, however, the relationship has been distant, uncertain, and even impersonal: now it becomes a face-to-face

---

8. *The Silver Chair*, 28.

9. *The Magician's Nephew*, 126-127.

10. Ibid., 114.

knowledge. Now is the time for Frank to learn to know Aslan by name, to look back on his life and to recognize who it was he had sensed near.

For many people who encounter Aslan in this way, there is one specific transaction that has to take place—that of apology and forgiveness.

Apology

In as far as the wrongs in the world of Narnia are the doing of people, one of the ways those wrongs are to be righted is by the people concerned taking responsibility for what they have done. They are expected to own up and admit their fault to Aslan—in religious language, they are to repent and confess their sins in order to be forgiven. The watchful dragons, of course, say this is a bad idea, humiliating and undignified. But they are wrong: apologies in Narnia bring renewed relationships, freedom and joy.

The earliest example is in *The Lion, the Witch and the Wardrobe*, when Peter, Susan and Lucy first meet Aslan. He asks why Edmund is not with them. They explain that Edmund has gone over to the Witch's side, but Peter quickly adds, "That was partly my fault, Aslan. I was angry with him and I think that helped him go wrong."[11] Often in our world, we are tempted to respond to such confessions by watering them down ("Oh, I'm sure you couldn't help it") or by adding our own reproaches ("How could you do such a thing?"). Aslan, however, simply accepts the statement, says nothing, and continues to look at Peter. Peter has said all that is needed. His words have power because of their simple truthfulness, and his relationship with Aslan is able to move forward. There is a similar confession when Jill admits to Aslan that her desire to show off caused Eustace to fall over the cliff and Aslan

---

11.   *The Lion, the Witch and the Wardrobe*, 118.

responds, without shock or condemnation, that this is "a very good answer."[12]

Lucy knows Aslan better than Jill does, and therefore, in *Prince Caspian*, when Lucy talks about her failure to persuade the other children to follow Aslan, once again he does not need to say anything. She works out for herself that she is partly responsible.

> "It wasn't my fault anyway, was it?"
> The Lion looked straight into her eyes.
> "Oh, Aslan," said Lucy. "You don't mean it was? How could I—I couldn't have left the others and come up to you alone, how could I? Don't look at me like that . . . oh well, I suppose I could . . ."
> Aslan said nothing.[13]

Lucy, naturally, having realized that she was in the wrong, wants to know what would have happened if she had obeyed. But once sin has been confessed, it is merely prurient to want to go back and think of what the alternatives might have been. Aslan's attitude is that once the wrongs of the past are dealt with, it is time to move on:

> "To know what might have happened, child? . . . Nobody is ever told that. . . . But anyone can find out what *will* happen."[14]

Confession is not a humiliating thing, making us less than we really are. But it is a humbling thing, acknowledging the truth of who we are: that we have not done what we ought to have done, or been what we should have been. In fact, in *The Horse and His Boy*, Bree is so embarrassed by his failure to defend Hwin and Aravis that he feels he is no longer worthy of Narnia and wants to return to Calormen to live as a slave. Aravis, with courage as well as spiritual insight, says it would be "better to stay and say we're sorry than to go back to Calormen."[15] In the

---

12. *The Silver Chair*, 27-28.
13. *Prince Caspian*, 124-125.
14. Ibid., 125.
15. *The Horse and His Boy*, 128.

short term, Aravis' proposal is the more costly one. Bree could stay in Calormen as a slave and nobody would ever have to know of his humiliation except himself.[16] But in the long run, to avoid apology is to avoid life and joy. Fortunately, when Bree meets Aslan, he takes Aravis' advice and acknowledges that he has been a fool. Aslan's response is typical: "Happy the Horse who knows that while he is still young. Or the Human either."[17]

Puzzle, the gullible donkey in *The Last Battle*, stands in contrast to Bree since he does not understand this principle. He is prepared to admit his error, but, unlike those who give proper apologies in Narnia, he tries to squirm out of personal responsibility by making excuses for himself. He blames Shift the Ape, he pleads his lack of intelligence, he explains that he didn't enjoy what he had been doing, and he tries to elicit pity by complaining that sometimes he got thirsty. He tells Tirian he is sorry "if" he has done wrong.

Perhaps the worst thing Puzzle says, however, is "I only did what I was told."[18] This sounds innocent enough—until one realizes that the same words were used by Nazis to excuse the atrocities they performed in World War II concentration camps. The Second World War ended in 1945. *The Last Battle* was written in 1956, when the memory of that war was still fresh, and war trials were still continuing. I suspect the verbal echo is deliberate.

It is Eustace (who once turned into a dragon in part because he would not take responsibility) who tries to confront Puzzle. It is no excuse for Puzzle to say he is not clever: he should have used what intelligence he actually has.[19] Jill, however, protects Puzzle and deflects the criticism: "It was all a mistake, wasn't it, Puzzle dear?" But Puzzle's complicity in

---

16.   The younger brother in Jesus' story could, I suppose, could have chosen to stay in the far country rather than return home and apologize. But then, he was hungry and Bree was not (Luke 15:11-24).

17.   *The Horse and his Boy*, 169.

18.   *The Last Battle*, 66.

19.   Ibid., 81.

the final war in Narnia is not "all a mistake"—Eustace is right to point out that he could have chosen differently—and Jill does him no favors by trying to gloss over the reality of what he has done.

Ultimately, of course, Puzzle, like everyone else, has to meet Aslan face to face:

> the Lion bowed down his head and whispered something to Puzzle at which his long ears went down; but then he said something else at which his ears perked up again. The humans couldn't hear what he had said either time.[20]

It may be presumptuous for humans to guess what was said by Aslan in private conversation, but presumably the words that caused Puzzle's ears to droop were words about his folly and guilt, and the words that caused him to perk up were words of forgiveness and reassurance: as so often happens with Aslan, bad news is closely followed by good news.

Here then is another characteristic Narnian theme: to tell the truth about what one has done wrong, without hiding it or excusing it, is the beginning of restoration. Confessing your sin, however painful it may seem at the time to look into those eyes of Aslan, is actually life-giving. Confession frees us from the past to move on into the future. And, more importantly, it brings us back into relationship with Aslan.

Any important truth can be expressed in more than one way, and the truth of the Deeper Magic is no exception. Certainly owning up to how we have contributed to the problems of Narnia and renewing our allegiance to Aslan is crucial. But Lewis offers other, more visual examples of how people (and animals, of course) can be redeemed. One is the story of what happens to the dragon formerly known as Eustace.

Transformation

While Eustace is still in his dragon state, late one night he meets Aslan, who leads him to a well in a garden on top of a mountain. There Eustace

---

20.   Ibid., 172.

wants to bathe but "the lion told me I must undress first." He scratches himself and finds that his dragon skin comes off. Underneath, however, he finds another dragon skin, and then another and yet another. When he finally despairs, Aslan tells him: "You will have to let me undress you." Aslan tears away the dragon skin completely, tearing so deeply "that I thought it had gone right into my heart." As a result, "it hurt worse than anything I've ever felt." Aslan then throws Eustace into the water, and he finds to his excitement, "I'd turned into a boy again."[21]

I find this a delightful image. Aslan's goal with us is not to make us peculiar or superhuman or even worse (as we might describe it in our world) "religious," but merely to restore our full humanity, to make us the person we were always meant to be. If one asks, "Why is sin wrong?" in Narnia at least the answer is that sin keeps us from being fully human, fully ourselves. But, as Eustace discovers, this is not something we can do without help, any more than we could cause ourselves to be born: we have to let Aslan do it for us. He is, after all, the Creator—and the Re-Creator.

There is another piece to the story of Eustace's restoration, however. Although owning up to Aslan puts right the vertical relationship (as it were), something has still to be done about the problems we have caused in horizontal relationships. Thus, when his encounter with Aslan is done, Eustace apologizes to Edmund, the first person he meets: "By the way, I'd like to apologize. I'm afraid I've been pretty beastly." Edmund's response is not to minimize or deny Eustace's "beastliness" but to acknowledge the truth of the confession—a response we may guess he learned from Aslan—and to share his own history of wrong-doing: "Between ourselves, you haven't been as bad as I was on my first trip to Narnia. You were only an ass, but I was a traitor."[22] Eustace is making significant progress. Having been reconciled to Aslan, he also takes steps to be reconciled to his fellow humans.

---

21. *The Voyage of the Dawn Treader*, 84-87.
22. Ibid., 87.

In this life, however, the distortion of our spirit caused by pride is never fully dealt with—like an injury that leaves us with a lifelong limp. The disease—our separation from Aslan—may be dealt with, but the symptoms continue. This is certainly true of Eustace. Lewis comments shrewdly:

> It would be nice, and fairly true, to say that "from that time forth Eustace was a different boy." To be strictly accurate, he began to be a different boy.[23]

As the *Dawn Treader* continues her voyage, some of the annoying traits we have seen in Eustace before his meeting with Aslan crop up again and again. Nevertheless, the important thing is that "the cure had begun."

---

23.   Ibid., 89.

9

"WE HEAR AND OBEY"

At the end of Eustace's undragoning, Lewis said of him, "the cure had begun." But is not only Eustace. For all of those who have joined Aslan's side, the cure has begun, but it has certainly not ended. Or, to change the analogy, there is much to be learned in the school of Aslan about how to live well and joyfully, and how to play our part in the story of his world.

We see two of the most important—and difficult—lessons being learned in two of the stories, *Prince Caspian* and *The Silver Chair*.

Seeing the Invisible

In *Prince Caspian*, the Pevensie children have been magicked from our world into Narnia once again, this time to come to the aid of Prince Caspian, the rightful king of Narnia, who is being besieged by the superior army of his uncle, the usurper King Miraz. First, however, they have to find Caspian.

At one point as they are travelling towards Caspian's camp, they come to the edge of a deep gorge, at the bottom of which is a river. It is not clear whether they should turn to right or left, but various factors incline them to think that right, down the hill, is the more direct. The oldest, Peter, begins to lead them down into the gorge. But before they can begin, Lucy sees Aslan—and he is telling them to go precisely the opposite way.[1] Unfortunately, nobody else has seen Aslan at this point (as Edmund points out elsewhere, it is Lucy who sees him most frequently[2]), and the majority vote to go with "common sense," against Lucy's advice, and to move down the gorge. God's commands—to love our neighbour as ourselves, to forgive our enemies, to confess our sins—seldom seem like common sense.

The one exception to the vote against Lucy is Edmund, who "speaking quickly and turning a little red," reminds the others that, when they first discovered Narnia, it was Lucy who was right when nobody else believed her and that in fact it was he, Edmund, who had been the most skeptical. Yet she had been right and the others wrong. Therefore, he asks, "Wouldn't it be fair to believe her this time? I vote for going up."[3] But Edmund is in the minority, so they set off, with Lucy bringing up the rear, "crying bitterly."[4] Going down the gorge, however, as we might have guessed, only leads them into an ambush set by Miraz' troops, and they have to retrace their steps uphill, hot, tired and thirsty, wasting energy and valuable time.

That night, once again, Aslan appears to Lucy, and once again she has to try to persuade the others to follow her as she follows Aslan. She naturally wants to know whether the others will be able to see him this time. "Certainly not at first," says Aslan. "Later on, it depends." Lucy complains that if they can't see him, they won't believe he is really there. But Aslan replies firmly, "It doesn't matter."[5]

Not surprisingly, it is Edmund who takes the lead this time in deciding to follow Lucy, and thus it is he who is the first to see that Aslan is indeed ahead of them on the path. At first he just sees a large shadow in front of them, but Lucy explains that it is Aslan's shadow, and Edmund says,

---

1. *Prince Caspian*, 110.
2. *The Voyage of the Dawn Treader*, 87.
3. *Prince Caspian*, 112.
4. Ibid., 113.
5. Ibid., 125.

"I can't think how I didn't see it before." We, however, can easily think why Edmund couldn't see. We often say "seeing is believing," but Lewis would say it is equally possible that "seeing is not believing."[6] Rather, our believing—and pursuing what we believe—leads to a certain way of seeing. It is a common mistake to think that "normal" people believe only what they see, whereas "religious" people somehow believe without the benefit of sight. The fact is that nobody believes only what they see. Everybody's "seeing" is governed by what they believe. If a person decides to be an atheist (a position of faith), they will see the world in a particular way. A person who decides to be a Zen Buddhist will see the world in quite a different way. Even the conviction that "seeing is believing" is itself a statement of faith which cannot be proved.

For Edmund, his commitment to follow Aslan means that slowly he comes to see the reality of Aslan. Sight follows believing, not the other way round. For Uncle Andrew in *The Magician's Nephew*, lack of belief meant he could not hear Aslan.[7] Now, for Edmund, belief (expressed by his following) means he can see Aslan. Our senses do not give us absolute truth: they are largely controlled by what we choose to believe or not to believe.

When the journey is over, and, one by one, they have all seen Aslan, Susan confesses to Lucy that she had really believed "deep down inside" that Lucy had seen Aslan the day before, and again when Lucy had woken them up to follow Aslan in the night. But somehow she had not allowed herself to believe, or to follow through on her belief that it was truly Aslan. She seems puzzled about her own actions, realizing that it was irrational not to follow through on what she believed.[8] Again, here is Lewis' emphasis on choice, but now it is tempered by an element of mystery. Something in Susan wanted to believe, drew her to believing. Yet it was as if a second Susan held the first one back, choosing not

---

6. "Miracles," in *God in the Dock*, 25. He is talking about a woman who claimed to have seen a ghost, but still did not believe in the immortality of the soul.

7. *The Magician's Nephew*, 117.

8. *Prince Caspian*, 132.

to believe and follow. Perhaps it was the voice of personal comfort (she wanted to get out of the woods). Perhaps it was the voice of fear, of wanting to avoid danger (Aslan says to her, "You have listened to fears, child"). In either case, her choice is not clear and thoughtful. As she ponders why she did what she did, she confesses that she really doesn't know. On one level, we never know why we choose not to follow, but the fact is, we often won't, even though we know it is right and good.[9]

Following the Maker's Instructions

The Silver Chair also explores the idea of following out of a sense of obedience. Jill and Eustace have been transported to Narnia to search for the missing Prince Rilian, heir to the throne. Aslan gives Jill four clues for finding him, and concludes: "[R]emember, remember, remember the signs." She is to recall them morning and night, and even if she wakes in the middle of the night. And, he adds, "whatever strange things happen to you, let nothing turn your mind from following the signs."[10]

Together with Puddleglum the Marshwiggle, Jill and Eustace trek through the wilderness in search of the lost prince, until they meet a beautiful woman on horseback who tells them they are not far from Harfang, the city of the gentle giants, where, she promises, they will be given warm hospitality. As a result, they begin to fantasize about that warm hospitality: all the comfortable beds, the warm baths and hot meals they will enjoy, compared with the hardships of their journey. These thoughts push all others out of their heads, thoughts of Aslan, thoughts of the prince for whom they are searching, and, most ominously of all, "Jill gave up her habit of repeating the signs over to herself every

---

9.   In the same way, in the first story, when Peter asks Edmund why he lied and said that Narnia was only a make-believe country, he stammers, "I thought—I thought," But as Peter rightly retorts, "You didn't think anything at all . . . it's just spite'" (*The Lion, the Witch and the Wardrobe*, 45). Socrates believed that if people know what is good they will do it. Lewis—and the Bible—would disagree.

10.   *The Silver Chair*, 30-31. There is a deliberate echo here of Moses' words to the people of Israel in Deuteronomy 6:6-9.

night and morning."[11] The lure of creature comforts has driven out of their heads the message they had been given. Their spirits may be willing to follow Aslan, but their flesh is weak. Good seeds had begun to grow, but the weeds of comfort and luxury have choked them. The call of obedience fades away as the sirens of warm hospitality turn up the volume.

It is Puddleglum, the real hero of this story, who remembers the importance of the clues: "Are you still sure of those signs, Pole? What's the one we ought to be after now?" But Jill has stopped caring. "Oh, come on! Bother the signs," she says. Of course, her annoyance is partly because she knows that Puddleglum is right: really the signs are more important than all the beds and baths in the world.[12]

As a result of this deliberate forgetfulness, they walk straight past the next clue in their hurry to arrive at Harfang before the gates close and they are shut out for the night. Having been welcomed by the giants, they go to bed. During the night, however, Aslan appears to Jill and shows her from her bedroom window the clue they missed. Eustace learned during the voyage of the *Dawn Treader* the lesson that it is liberating to admit your failings, and so is quick to confess where he went wrong: they were so eager to get to the castle that they forgot everything else. "We must just own up," he concludes. Jill too has imbibed this spirit of "owning up" and so when Eustace moans that they have messed up the signs, she corrects him: "You mean I have. ... It's quite true."[13]

The castle, of course, far from being the haven they had expected, turns out to be a death trap: the giants regard human beings as a great delicacy for the forthcoming Autumn Feast. The luxury the Queen of the Underworld promised meant death; the hardship that came with obeying Aslan meant life. They manage to escape from the giants, but of course they cannot put the clock back to the time before they entered

---

11. Ibid., 84.
12. Ibid., 91.
13. Ibid., 85-86.

the gate of Harfang and undo their disobedience. No-one can know what might have happened, but "anyone can find out what *will* happen", as Aslan tells Lucy on another occasion.[14] And what does happen is that they are able to redeem their mistake and to find Prince Rilian.

The theme of difficult obedience takes a further turn when the three finally find the prince. While he is under an evil enchantment, the prince tells them that a fit comes over him at night, so that every night he is bound to a silver chair. He warns that they might be tempted to untie him, but that whatever he says, however he pleads, they should not do so. Of course, he says this while enchanted. The truth is that the Queen wants him to be restrained at night because that is when he is himself, and it is she who has taught him the opposite. As a result, that night, while he is bound to the chair and free of the enchantment, he pleads with them to release him . . . in the name of Aslan. What are they to do? The fourth clue was that they would recognize the prince by the fact that he would be the first person they had met who would ask them to do something in Aslan's name![15]

Surely this is the sign they have been looking for? Yet they cannot be sure which persona of the prince is the true one. If the warning the prince gave them during the day is true, then releasing him from the silver chair will mean certain death.

> "Oh, if only we knew!" said Jill.
> "I think we do know," said Puddleglum.

What he knows is that the choice is not between safety and danger. The real choice is between obedience and disobedience, and as far as Puddleglum is concerned, that is no choice at all. Eustace wonders whether untying the prince will mean that everything will turn out right, but of course it is not as simple as that, as Puddleglum realizes. Aslan had made no promises about the outcome: he merely told them what to do.

---

14. *Prince Caspian*, 125.
15. *The Silver Chair*, 29.

Puddleglum's usual pessimism seems justified for once: "That fellow will be the death of us once he's up, I shouldn't wonder. But that doesn't let us off following the sign."[16]

Puddleglum understands rightly that obedience to Aslan never guarantees safety or happiness. But obeying is the right thing to do, because he is the king.[17] In fact, their gamble pays off: they free Prince Rilian and together the four of them return to Narnia. Puddleglum's insight remains valid, however: obedience is right because of who gives the command, not because the outcome is certain.

These seem to be the two fundamental principles of living in Narnia: trust and obey. They sound simple, even simplistic. And obedience in particular has a bad press in our world: to obey someone is to lose your independence and your individuality. We associate it with policemen and wicked dictators. Yet most of us have actually experienced a positive side to obedience: perhaps in a teacher who really cared for us and wanted to bring out the best in us, and whom we loved to obey, even when it was difficult. This is the kind of obedience that operates in Narnia: to trust and obey Aslan, who knows all things, who made you, loves you and desires the best for you, is actually liberating, whereas "doing your own thing" is what leads to trouble. To trust and obey will lead you through all sorts of adventures, help you become who you are meant to be, and bring you joy.[18]

Aslan's work in us, however, is often slow and difficult. Old ways of thinking and feeling linger on. New ways take time to put down roots and bear fruit. Eustace offers a case study of how change slowly takes place, and how small victories are to be applauded.

---

16. Ibid., 145.

17. Lewis writes elsewhere about the First Servant in Shakespeare's *King Lear*, who does what is right and gets killed for his pains. He only speaks eight lines in the play. Yet, says Lewis, "if it were real life and not a play, that is the part it would be best to have acted" ("The World's Last Night," in *Fern-seeds and Elephants*, 76).

18. Lewis quotes Montaigne with approval: "to obey is the proper office of a rational soul" (*A Preface to Paradise Lost* [Oxford University Press, 1942; 1977], 76).

How Eustace changes

After the undragoning of Eustace, as the voyage of the *Dawn Treader* continues, we see just what Lewis had in mind when he said that Eustace began to be a different boy but still "had relapses" when he could be "very tiresome."[19]

For example, Eustace is still competitive, which Lewis says is the essence of pride: "Pride is *essentially* competitive—is competitive by its very nature."[20] Thus when Eustace lost to Reepicheep at chess, he "began to get rather like his old and disagreeable self again."[21] Or again: he still has the kind of mind that enjoys facts and figures and is imaginatively challenged. Thus, on the Island of the Voices, when they see a pump at work without any hand working it, while most friends of Narnia would assume magic was at work, Eustace sees it as a sign that they have at last returned to civilization.[22] Old habits of mind are still at work. At Ramandu's table, he is still the practical Eustace, asking how the food keeps, and informing Ramandu that in our world "a star is a huge ball of flaming gas."[23] Even at the end of the book, when Caspian learns to his delight that the children's world is round (round worlds are the stuff of myths in Narnia), Eustace still wants to argue that worlds cannot be flat—even Narnia.[24]

But there are changes. When the *Dawn Treader* is attacked by the sea serpent, Eustace does "the first brave thing he had ever done," drawing Caspian's second best sword and attacking the serpent. The serpent is impervious to his blows, but "it was a fine thing for a beginner to have done," and everyone is impressed and compliments him on his bravery.[25] The old Eustace would never have done such a deed, but the air of

19. *The Voyage of the Dawn Treader*, 99.
20. *Mere Christianity*, 107.
21. *The Voyage of the Dawn Treader*, 100.
22. Ibid., 116.
23. Ibid., 171, 177.
24. Ibid., 95.
25. Ibid., 102, 105.

Narnia, and indeed the spirit of Aslan, are slowly having their way with him. Perhaps more dramatically, he volunteers to stay the night at Ramandu's table, despite his fears. Lewis points out that those who had read stories of magic and enchantment had an advantage when it came to facing such tests, since they knew that usually these things work out well. Eustace, on the other hand, having read the wrong books, did not have the same assurance of the outcome, and therefore was actually braver than the other children.[26]

Not only is he learning new ways of thinking and acting: there is also a sense that the old ways of being are loosening their hold on him. So when the *Dawn Treader* continues to sail east day after day, and even experienced sailors are worrying, Eustace agrees that they are "crazy." Then Lewis adds that he only said this from old habit and not in the nasty way he would once have done.[27] The habit of skepticism continues, but somehow the edge has gone off it. It is as though the wound is still healing—but from time to time it still itches. In time the scab will drop away and the healing will be complete—though probably not until Eustace is in Aslan's world.

For obvious reasons, it is a little difficult to compare creators of worlds! But, if we could, I suspect that some, seeing the world they made go wrong in the way that Narnia does, would give up on it, scrap the failed creation, and start over. Aslan however is not that kind of Creator. Little by little, he begins to restore his crippled world. The climax, which he planned from the beginning, is his death at the hands of the White Witch. But then he seeks out individuals, draws them into his friendship, shares his plans and his work with them, and slowly transforms them to be the people he created them to be.

The consummation of Aslan's redemption of Narnia and its people, however, is yet to come, and happens outside of time. This brings us to fifth question: Where are we going?

---

26. Ibid., 166-167.
27. Ibid., 106.

10

NARNIA IS DEAD, LONG LIVE NARNIA!

I once walked around wearing sandwich boards which proclaimed, "The end of the world is at hand." I have to admit I was not making a serious statement—at least, not about the end of the world. I was in a church in Ottawa speaking about evangelism, and I wanted to begin by demonstrating how silly Christians can look when engaged in some forms of evangelism.

Yet every Big Story offers some kind of belief about the end of the world, though few seem to believe it is "at hand." My guess is that the majority of people, certainly in the West, believe that human life on this planet will continue either until there is an ecological disaster (probably caused by us) which will wipe us out, or until our sun cools sufficiently that life becomes impossible.

The Christian tradition from which Lewis came has by and large not believed this is the way the world will end. Although there have been significant variations, basic Christian belief has been that at the end of time, Jesus will return to wrap up history, judging the inhabitants of the world, distributing rewards and punishments, and ushering in a new world. Some understand Jesus to have foretold a time of particular evil just before the end, perhaps headed up by a figure called the Antichrist. Lewis was not very concerned about the details of the end, but he certainly believed the basic contention of Christian spirituality that Jesus "will come again to judge the living and the dead"[1] and to bring down the curtain on the history of our world.

This being so, it is not surprising that in the Narnian world of "supposals" he would suppose what might happen at the end of that world's life. It is time to look at *The Last Battle*.

Lewis has traveled a long way in his thinking since *The Lion, the Witch and the Wardrobe*. Here, in *The Last Battle*, his thinking on a number of subjects comes together to complete "the big picture." Here, for example, we see that the world's problems are not just something played out on the human stage, but rather involve cosmic forces beyond our comprehension. We learn as a corollary that our choices in this life have consequences which extend beyond this life. Yet the fundamental lesson of *The Lion, the Witch and the Wardrobe*, that the most important thing about a person is whether he or she is a servant of Aslan, still undergirds everything else.

The end of the old Narnia

Two new animal characters meet us in the opening pages of *The Last Battle*. Each presents us with a face of evil we have not yet seen. Shift the Ape is perhaps the most unpleasant character in the Chronicles. From the very first page, he is portrayed as self-centered and manipulative, thinking only of his own ease and comfort. Although he pretends friendship with Puzzle the donkey, Puzzle is in fact virtually his slave. Add to this, however, the fact that Shift cares nothing about Aslan, and is willing to twist others' belief in Aslan to his own ends, and the coloring of the picture becomes significantly darker.

Shift's "friend," Puzzle, also sheds a new light on evil. He is certainly innocent and naïve, easily convinced by Shift's arguments that he, Puzzle, should do something more for Shift's comfort or pleasure. But by the middle of the book his seeming innocence is no longer so attrac-

---

1. The Apostles' Creed.

tive or pitiable. There is something quite sinister in the picture of the gentle donkey dressed up in the bedraggled skin of a lion, silhouetted by a flickering campfire. In fact, he is seen to be culpable. It is true that he has been used by Shift, but he could have taken more responsibility for his actions; he did not need to let himself be used to the extent that he was.

Yet there is more here than just new characters. As the story unfolds, we become aware of the reality of huge cosmic powers lurking behind the appearance of human good and evil. The conflict between good and evil is no longer one that can be resolved by sincere apology and asking Aslan's forgiveness. This book describes war. Nor does this story have a happy ending—in Narnia, at least. (In another sense, it has the ultimate happy ending.) King Tirian is consistently referred to as the last king of Narnia, and in the final battle, nearly all of those on the side of Narnia are killed. The stakes in the conflict of good and evil are very high indeed.

The story opens with Shift and Puzzle discovering the skin of a dead lion. Shift proposes that Puzzle should wear the skin and pretend to be Aslan, in order to put right all the wrongs with which Narnia is afflicted. When thunder from heaven warns them against such a strategy, Puzzle understands it correctly ("I knew we were doing something dreadfully wicked"), but Shift is quick to reinterpret it as a sign of Aslan's affirmation ("No, no. It's a sign the other way").[2] The "blasphemy against the Holy Spirit," against which Jesus warned, was to say that good is evil and evil good.[3] This is precisely what Shift does.

Pretending to have Aslan's authority behind him, he makes an agreement with the neighbouring country of Calormen for them to fell and remove Narnian trees ("holy trees"), to use Narnian talking animals for slave labour, and to transport the Dwarfs of Narnia to work in the mines of Calormen. Shift keeps the pliable Puzzle in a small,

---

2.   *The Last Battle*, 17.

3.   Mark 3:28-30.

dark stable, and only brings him out at night, by the uncertain light of a bonfire, to add the supposed authority of Aslan to his commands.

Here is the abuse of power which Aslan sought to guard against in the commission he gave to the first king and queen of Narnia: power being used for personal gain rather than for the good of others, power which lacks respect for people, animals and trees.[4] It had been a sign of Narnia's health centuries earlier when the four kings and queens "made good laws and kept the peace and saved good trees from being unnecessarily cut down."[5] But those days are over now.

In Narnia, it has always been important for people and animals to know who or what they are, and to fulfill the role to which Aslan has called them. It is thus a sign of the Ape's sinfulness that he wants to be something other than himself. He tells the other animals he is not really an ape but a man. The reason he looks like an ape is because he is centuries old.[6] People in Narnia begin to go wrong when they begin to behave like "beasts."[7] Beasts, on the other hand, are in trouble when they start wanting to be human. Long before this, Mr. Beaver, speaking of the Witch, who wanted to be human but was not, had warned the children to be on the lookout for anything "that's going to be human, and isn't yet, or used to be human once and isn't now, or ought to be human and isn't."[8] He might have added to his list, "anything that is an animal but pretends to be a human," for the principle is the same. This deception on the Ape's part compounds his folly.

As the tragedy unfolds, there is an even worse way in which the reality Aslan has built into the nature of Narnia is challenged and distorted. The line between good and evil becomes blurred. The religions of Narnia and Calormen are now said to be the same:

---

4. *The Last Battle*, 24.

5. *The Lion, the Witch and the Wardrobe*, 166.

6. *The Last Battle*, 33.

7. E.g., *The Lion, the Witch and the Wardrobe*, 45, 46, 55, 139.

8. Ibid., 77.

"Tash is only another name for Aslan. . . . The Calormenes use different words but we all mean the same thing."[9]

The loving creator god who is Aslan is incorporated into the cruel and destructive god Tash. Tirian rightly questions how this can be possible, when Tash is known to drink the blood of his followers, while Aslan shed his blood so that Narnia could be saved. They hardly sound like the same god when their behaviour is so opposite.[10] But Tirian is quickly silenced. Of course, once good and evil, truth and falsehood, are obliterated, even in the name of tolerance, all that is actually left is unprincipled power—and that the Ape is determined to wield.

However, it is a consistent principle of Lewis' spirituality that "All find what they truly seek."[11] Those who claim to be servants of Tash will find him. Those who seek Aslan, though it may be by a different name, will also find their heart's desire. Thus, at the end of the story, to the surprise of some of his "believers," Tash comes to claim his own. The Ape who claimed to represent Tash but did not really believe in Tash's existence "will get more than he bargained for! He called for Tash: Tash has come."[12] And the evil Tash devours both Shift and Rishda Tarkaan, leader of the Calormene forces.

The fear of Tash also turns Ginger the scheming cat back into a dumb animal. When Narnia was created, Aslan had chosen some of the creatures to be Talking Beasts, but he had also warned them that if they turned to evil, their power of speech could be taken away. Ginger, in his unbelief, may have been on the side of Tash, but his punishment is not from Tash: what happens to Ginger when he loses the power of speech is simply that the words of Aslan, spoken thousands of years before, are fulfilled.[13] There is a ghastly appropriateness about what happens: if

---

9. *The Last Battle*, 35.
10. Ibid., 37.
11. Ibid., 156.
12. Ibid., 80.
13. Ibid., 105.

Ginger separates himself from the source of his power to speak, then he will not be able to speak. It is a punishment of sorts, but an inevitable and "natural" one.

As the forces of Calormen gradually overwhelm the small group of defenders of Narnia, one by one they throw them in through the door of the stable, there to meet Tash—as they think. But once inside the door, the children find to their amazement that they are in Aslan's country, away from the noise and the darkness, the fear and the fighting.

Then Aslan steps in and with his cry of "Now it is time!"[14] brings things to an end—not just the battle between the Narnians and the Calormenes, but all of Narnia and its history. The giant Father Time awakens from his underground sleep, and blows his horn to signal the end. The stars fall until the sky is empty, and all the creatures of Narnia begin to stream towards the huge doorway where Aslan stands.[15] Then comes the final judgement—but in Lewis' portrayal it is significantly different from the traditional picture (such as Michelangelo's scene on the wall of the Sistine Chapel in Rome), where the Judge decides what will happen to each person. In the Narnian version, in one sense Aslan does nothing. Certainly he says nothing. As each animal approaches him, they look at him ("I don't think they had any choice about that"). As some of them look, fear and even hatred cross their face, and they turn to their right (Aslan's left) and disappear into his shadow. But others look into his face, and their expression is filled with love, even though some are clearly afraid at the same time. These enter the door on Aslan's right.[16]

The judgment, in other words, is what the animals have chosen for themselves. When they are confronted with Aslan, the ultimate symbol of good and of God, the reality that has grown and been nurtured in their hearts over their lifetime becomes visible on their faces. Some know, as

---

14.   Ibid., 141.

15.   Ibid., 142-144.

16.   Ibid., 146. This distinction between left and right derives from Jesus' own picture of the last judgment, where indeed the Judge does pronounce the verdict (Matthew 25:31-45).

they look on Aslan, that this is what they have been searching for all of their lives. Others realize that this is what they have been trying to avoid and hide from all of their lives. None who truly want to enter Aslan's new world are turned away. None who hate Aslan and what he stands for are forced to enter.

Entering the new Narnia

What happens next? Every Big Story says something about "what happens next." Perhaps the end of the human race is simply annihilation, so that for the individual at least nothing happens next: there is no "next." On this theory, there may well be a future for the race, though the likelihood is that one day even the race will cease to exist. Other Big Stories speak of reincarnation, and the eventual merging of the individual into universal consciousness. Yet others speak of a heaven which seems cloudy and vague, and somehow less interesting, less real, than this world.

If Lewis were to choose, he would choose the last as closest to the teaching of Jesus and Christian tradition. But he had no time for a heaven that was less real than this world, and his picture of the new Narnia tries to convey the super-reality of the next world.

Personally, I find his picture of the new Narnia one of the most moving passages in all of literature. For many years, I used to teach a course on the Christian worldview to teenagers at a summer camp, often using videos and stories to illustrate it. When it came to the last of the worldview questions—where are we going?—I would always read the description of Aslan's world at the end of *The Last Battle.* But I always found it (and still do) intensely moving, and could hardly get through it without my voice breaking. Over the years, however, I found a solution: I drew happy faces in the margin every few lines, and somehow the glimpse of a silly happy face kept me from feeling the full emotional force of what I was reading. But even so, when I am just reading it to myself, I still feel the impact. I once heard it read at a funeral, and I think everybody was in tears.[17]

I think this part of the story affects people this way because Lewis' picture of Aslan's land is in many ways, not just emotionally, the climax of the Chronicles. It is, as he says himself, the place of the Great Story to which all the other stories have been leading us.[18] What can be said of this place? Maybe the most important thing is that Aslan's land does not replace the old Narnia: it fulfils the old Narnia.[19] To the children's amazement and delight, they find that everything they had ever loved is present in this new world, not just the people and the animals but also the places. As Lewis once said in a sermon, it is as though what they had experienced in the rest of their lives up to this point was an orchestral piece arranged for piano: it was beautiful and memorable and haunting, but only now as they hear the score played by the full orchestra do they realize the dimensions of that beauty they had been missing before.[20] This is the sense in which the new Narnia is "deeper [and] means more" than the old one, is "more like the real thing."

This is Lewis' clearest picture of the next life. His friend George Sayer says that, for Lewis, heaven was:

---

17.   I find it reassuring that Lewis himself "lost his composure" while preaching a sermon entitled "Transposition" on this very subject (Paul F. Ford, "The Voyage of the Dawn Treader," in Schultz and West, 420).

18.   *The Last Battle,* 173.

19.   I am aware that some Christians dislike the Platonism (which the professor makes explicit) in this scene, because historically Platonism in Christianity has led to a false understanding of what "spiritual" means and to a devaluing of the physicality of this world. They would therefore stress the renewal of this world at the end of time, rather than its replacement or even fulfillment in the new creation. Although he clearly does believe in the destruction of the old Narnia and the creation of a new one, Lewis actually has a higher view of the materiality of both worlds than the charge of Platonism might suggest. He says, for example, "[God] likes matter. He invented it." *Mere Christianity,* 62. He also sees the next world as more real than this one, not less. See, for example, the description in *The Great Divorce.*

20.   "Transposition" in *Screwtape Proposes a Toast,* 81.

a place where all sorts of people could come together to celebrate, dance, and sing with fauns, giants, centaurs, dwarfs, and innumerable and very different animals.[21]

It is that, but it is also more than that. Here people stop getting older, and suffering has come to an end. Digory says that he and Polly "felt that we'd been unstiffened . . . we stopped feeling old." Though Digory's beard was white in the first story,[22] it has now turned back from white to its original gold.[23] They find too that "time there is not like time here," so they can no longer tell whether things are taking a long or short time.[24] Maybe this is why Father Time receives a new name in this world.[25] Even fear has disappeared, and situations that might once have caused fear now merely cause excitement: "Have you noticed one can't feel afraid, even if one wants to?" asks Lucy.[26]

More significantly, sin has ceased to exist. There is no treachery, no pride; all relationships are healed and restored, with Aslan, one another, and the creation. As a result, there is no longer the possibility of doing wrong, or even of wanting to do wrong. When the children are unsure as to whether they can eat the fruit of Aslan's country, Peter rightly says, "I've a feeling we've got to the country where everything is allowed."[27]

Lewis is careful to say that this picture of heaven is not a complete one: he is wiser than to try to describe such a thing. The clue is in the refrain so frequently repeated, "Farther up and farther in!" What he

---

21. *Jack*, 316.

22. *The Lion, the Witch and the Wardrobe*, 9.

23. *The Last Battle*, 132.

24. Ibid., 169.

25. Ibid., 142.

26. Ibid., 164.

27. Ibid., 130. A scene in an earlier book foreshadows this: Caspian asks whether it is legitimate for him to want a glimpse of our world, and Aslan reassures him: "You cannot want wrong things any more, now that you have died, my son" (*The Silver Chair*, 204).

describes here are only the outskirts, the suburbs, of heaven. What lies "farther in" cannot be conceived or described; indeed those things are "so great and beautiful that I cannot write them."[28] But there is enough in what he does tell us to arouse our longing and touch our hearts. Many of us, reading this, find we want to echo the words of Jewel the Unicorn: "This is the land I have been looking for all my life, though I never knew it till now."[29]

It is no coincidence that Lewis uses similar language about his rediscovery of joy after some years away: "[T]here arose at once . . . the knowledge that . . . I was returning at last from exile and desert lands to my own country."[30] Yet the final goal of joy is Aslan's country, our true home. In his portrait of the new Narnia, Lewis is wanting us to look for it and long for it, even if it takes the whole of our lives, because he knows it is what we were made for.

28.   Ibid., 173.
29.   Ibid., 162.
30.   *Mere Christianity*, 62.

11

ALL FIND WHAT
THEY TRULY SEEK

At the end of fairy stories, we are assured, everybody "lives happily ever after." Maybe that reflects a certain kind of Big Story of the universe: those who do well and conquer all obstacles, especially if it is in the name of love, will be rewarded with everlasting happiness. But that is not Lewis' view. He certainly believes that we have the possibility of living happily ever after, but he believes equally that we may choose not to do so. If that seems strange, consider who is present in Aslan's country—and who is not. And why.

The Dwarfs

One of the clearest examples is the Dwarfs, who, although they find themselves in Aslan's land, cannot be persuaded to live happily ever after. While everyone else is enjoying its beauty, the Dwarfs sit in a circle, believing they are still in the dark, smelly stable. Lucy is distressed by their folly. Surely Aslan can help? But even Aslan's power is limited by their determination to say no to joy. He spreads a splendid feast in front of them: yet still they think they are eating garbage from the stable.

What is their problem? Is it not the desire of every heart to find Aslan's country? Apparently not. The Dwarfs have already shown that they have other priorities in their lives. Much earlier, when Tirian showed them that the false Aslan was only Puzzle in a lion skin, he assumed the Dwarfs would be delighted, and flock to his banner. But they are suspicious. Why should they believe Tirian's story any more than the Calormenes'?[1] So what is it that motivates them if not the desire for Aslan's country? They make no secret of it. They are simply going to look after themselves and ignore everything and everyone else: "The Dwarfs are for the Dwarfs."[2]

During the final battle, they repeat this refrain more than once. They use their arrows with deadly accuracy to destroy whichever side seems to have the advantage. They don't care who is right and who is wrong: they are only interested in self-preservation. They jeer when Eustace expresses outrage at their immoral behaviour. They don't want anyone to win except themselves. And they are certainly not going to be taken in by anyone.[3] Which side are you on? Where will you throw your efforts? For Tash or for Aslan? The Dwarfs' reply is neither. The Dwarfs are for the Dwarfs.

In some ways, this sounds very sensible. Why should they not "look after number one"? In the reality of Narnia, however, this is a dangerous approach to things. The way that gives life in Narnia is actually counterintuitive: it is not self-preservation but the way of self-giving. You have to give away your life in order to find it: if you try to save your life you will lose it.[4] Aslan modelled that at the beginning of Narnia, when he said, "I give you myself."[5] And he demonstrated it supremely when he surrendered his life to the knife of the White Witch so that Edmund might live.

---

1. *The Last Battle*, 71. In modern parlance, we might say they exercise a hermeneutic of suspicion.

2. Ibid., 72-72.

3. Ibid., 117.

4. Cf. Jesus' words in Mark 8:35.

5. *The Magician's Nephew*, 109.

This is the grain of the universe as Aslan has shaped it: to go against that grain is to go counter to the nature of reality, and to court unreality.

When we meet the Dwarfs again in the outskirts of Aslan's land, this unreality has finally overtaken them. They have refused help and therefore cannot be helped. As Aslan puts it, "Their prison is only in their own minds, yet they are in that prison."[6] Even now, if they had stretched out a hand for help, they would have received it: but they would never ask. Their constant insistence that they are for themselves alone has become so automatic a response, so hard-wired into them, that there is no longer any possibility of change. They are willingly trapped inside their own illusion of a dark, dirty stable even though it no longer exists. This is the dangerous side of the gift we so value called freedom.

Not all stories have so gloomy a conclusion, however. The story of what happens to Susan seems at first sight to be just as pessimistic as that of the Dwarfs, but in Lewis' mind at least her story may yet have a happy ending.

Susan

There are three indications in the Chronicles of what is to come in the story of Susan, though the third is probably the most significant.

Throughout the book, Susan is the most timid of the four siblings. When they first enter Narnia, she is the one who is worried about the danger and is not sure they should stay. This new country doesn't look to her as though it is safe or even fun, and she wants them all to go home.[7] At the end of *The Lion, the Witch and the Wardrobe*, even after years in Narnia, she experiences the same kind of fear once again. They are pursuing the fabled White Stag, but it leads them to a strange iron pole with a light on the top which causes an unfamiliar response in

---

6.   *The Last Battle*, 140-141. Uncle Andrew similarly shuts out Aslan's desire to give him joy (*The Magician's Nephew*, 158).

7.   *The Lion, the Witch and the Wardrobe*, 57.

them. The others are all for exploring further, but Susan is nervous and urges them to go back, for fear of what adventures might await them.[8]

Thus her fears form bookends to *The Lion, the Witch and the Wardrobe*. In both cases, of course, what she is afraid of is risk and adventure, and Narnia is full of both. In the same way, it is Susan who is afraid to venture into the cellar of the ruined Cair Paravel early in *Prince Caspian*.[9] In that same book, Lewis describes her as "the practical Susan,"[10] and in Narnia, as we have already observed, this is not a compliment: it implies a lack of the imagination and daring which make life worth living.

The second thing I notice—and it may be only coincidence that it is Susan in this incident—is that she is the one who questions the ways of the Emperor-beyond-the-Sea. When Aslan explains that treachery must be punished by death, she is the one who asks whether there isn't anything that can be done to counteract the Deep Magic. Aslan responds with "something like a frown on his face" and asks, "Work against the Emperor's Magic?"[11]

Perhaps, at this early stage of their relationship with Aslan, any one of the children could have made this comment, implying that the Emperor's way is not as good as their own. But it may also be that Lewis is preparing us for the fact that at the end of Narnia, Susan is the one who will be missing.

Alongside these characteristics, there is a third thing: Susan is the one of the four who behaves and talks most like a grown-up. Almost as soon as the stories begin, she suggests that it is Edmund's bed-time, and he immediately retorts, "Stop trying to talk like Mother."[12] It is an innocent enough thing in any family for the oldest girl to take on characteristics of her mother. But in Susan's case it easily turns into being patronizing. In *Prince Caspian*, when Lucy is the only one who can see Aslan, Susan asks

---

8.   Ibid., 169.

9.   *Prince Caspian*, 26.

10.   Ibid., 107.

11.   *The Lion, the Witch and the Wardrobe*, 129.

12.   Ibid., 10.

in an annoyingly grown-up way: "Where did you think you saw him?"[13] Being grown-up and trusting Lucy's vision seem to work at odds with one another.

This is the trait which in the end seems to have distracted her from Narnia. Peter says curtly: "My sister Susan . . . is no longer a friend of Narnia." Jill explains that Susan has become more interested in nothing but "nylons and lipstick and invitations." Then she adds, "She always was a jolly sight too keen on being grown-up."[14] One might be forgiven for thinking that typical adolescent interests are hardly a strong enough reason to be excluded from Aslan's country: aren't such things just a normal part of Susan's growing up?[15] Certainly.

The more significant part of what has happened to Susan, however, is her desire to be a particular kind of grown-up. For C. S. Lewis, this kind of grown-up has no imagination, and has lost the ability to dream and risk and change. For him, that is almost the unforgivable sin. Not because it is a criminal offence to be grown-up. No: Lewis is more subtle than that. Once again, it is to do with the choices we make.

In his thinking, people who are too "grown-up" in this sense have chosen to place themselves outside the redemptive power of Narnia. The reason they cannot be forgiven is because they will not take advantage of the forgiveness that is offered. The clue that this is what is happening with Susan is what Eustace quotes her as saying: "Fancy your still thinking about all those funny games we used to play when we were children."[16] Once again, it is worth quoting Lewis' central con-

---

13.   *Prince Caspian*, 111.

14.   *The Last Battle*, 129.

15.   Lewis' goddaughter, Sarah Tisdall, says, "I was very hurt when Susan was banished from Narnia because she liked lipstick. I felt that might be me" ("A Goddaughter's Memories" in *C. S Lewis Remembered: Collected Reflections of Students, Friends and Colleagues*, ed. Harry Lee Poe and Rebecca Whitten Poe [Grand Rapids: Zondervan, 2006], 221).

16.   *The Last Battle*, 129.

viction in his life and his faith that "all find what they truly seek."[17] As he writes elsewhere:

> I think that whatever she had seen in Narnia she could (if she was the sort that wanted to) persuade herself, as she grew up, that it was 'all nonsense'.[18]

Thus, if Susan is no longer seeking Narnia, she will of course not find Narnia.

Is this then the end for Susan, cut off for ever from Aslan? Lewis was not willing to go that far. A boy called Martin wrote to him to ask what happened to Susan in the end. Lewis' answer is revealing:

> The books don't tell us what happened to Susan. She is left alive in this world at the end, having by then turned into a rather silly, conceited young woman. But there is plenty of time for her to mend, and perhaps she will get to Aslan's country in the end—in her own way.[19]

As Aslan himself has told us, he is known by another name in our world, and it may be that Susan will encounter him as a "grown-up" by that name rather than by the name Aslan—as Lewis himself did. Lewis has clearly not given up hope for Susan.

One might have expected Susan to be in Aslan's country along with the rest of the children—but she is not. But equally there are people in Aslan's country we might have expected not to be there. For instance, Eustace spots coming through the door to Aslan's right one of the Dwarfs who just a short time before had been shooting the horses. Presumably he is a Dwarf who was willing "to be taken out."[20] Clearly we do not know what really goes on in people's relationship with Aslan, and, as Lewis points out, it was no business of Eustace's. This is presumably why

---

17.   Ibid., 156.
18.   *Letters to Children*, 67.
19.   Ibid., 67.
20.   *The Last Battle*, 146.

Aslan tells Shasta, "I tell nobody any story but their own."[21] But there is one person in Aslan's land whom we do not expect to be there, and who tells us his own story: his name is Emeth.

Emeth

As the children begin to explore Aslan's country, they discover a Calormene soldier. Surely he should not be there? After all, he was a soldier of Tash who fought on the side of evil against Aslan.

Emeth (for that is who it is) is in some ways as puzzled as they are as to why he is there, but he tells them his story. He had served Tash all his life and, he says, "my great desire was to know more of him."[22] So, when he was told that Tash was in the stable on the hill, and saw the dramatic effect that entering the stable had on the cat Ginger, he decided that come what may he too would go into the stable to meet his god "though he should slay me."[23] The Narnians had in fact noticed Emeth entering the stable at the time with a look of solemn joy on his face, and Jewel had commented, "I almost love this young warrior . . . He is worthy of a better god than Tash."[24]

Once inside the stable, however, Emeth does not meet Tash: instead he meets the Lion. Naturally, he is terrified, since Aslan will know that he has served Tash all of his life. But to his amazement, Aslan greets him as a son. When Emeth corrects him, admitting that he is the servant of Tash and not a child of Aslan, Aslan contradicts him: "all the service thou hast done to Tash, I account as service done to me." Emeth dares to ask how this is possible, and Aslan replies: "no service which is vile can be done to me, and none which is not vile can be done to him." To keep a promise made in the name of Tash is actually pleasing to Aslan, not to Tash, simply because Aslan affirms all integrity; while

---

21.   *The Horse and his Boy*, 139.

22.   *The Last Battle*, 153.

23.   Ibid., 154. Cf., Job 13:15, "Though he slay me, yet will I hope in him."

24.   Ibid., 108.

to break a promise, even if it is made in the name of Aslan, is actually pleasing to Tash, but not to Aslan.[25] Thus Emeth thinks he has been serving Tash, but, since Tash represents the power of evil, when Emeth did right, Tash rejected it, but Aslan took notice. He has actually been serving Aslan without knowing it.

Is Lewis saying that all religions are the same? That it really does not matter what you believe, and everybody who is sincere gets to heaven in the end? This would be a superficial interpretation and would contradict what he says elsewhere. Let me say first of all that Lewis is clearly not one of those Christians who believe that every other religion is totally wrong (though he does note that atheists have to believe so). At the same time, he is equally clear that:

> where Christianity differs from other religions, Christianity is right
> and they are wrong. As in arithmetic—there is only one right answer
> to a sum, and all other answers are wrong; but some of the wrong
> answers are much nearer to being right that others.[26]

He makes this strong-sounding claim, not because he is intolerant, but simply because of his conviction that Jesus is the fulfillment of the longings of all philosophies, mythologies and religions.[27] For instance, to take one of Lewis' favourite examples, the myth of the corn god who dies and rises again contains some aspects of truth—but in Jesus, God the Creator really does die and rise again at a point in history.[28] Thus Jesus does not so much contradict other religions as fulfill them: and in the same way Aslan fulfils the heart's longing of a noble follower of Tash.

Emeth has been seeking for truth (it is surely significant that his name means "truth" in Hebrew) all of his life. He thought truth was to be found in Tash, but in fact the ultimate truth he was seeking was to be found

---

25. Ibid., 156.

26. *Mere Christianity*, 39.

27. "[I]n Christ whatever is true in all religions is consummated and perfected" ("Christian Apologetics," in *God in the Dock*, 102).

28. E.g., "Miracles" in *God in the Dock*, 37.

only in Aslan. He could not know that, however, because his culture did not teach him the true nature of Aslan.

Thus Lewis is not saying anything quite as inclusive as it might at first sound. He is actually saying something quite tough-minded: that wherever people are truly seeking for truth, they will only find it when they find Aslan. And when they meet Aslan face to face, they will know that it is he they have been seeking. This is why, when Emeth finally encounters Aslan, he says: "it is better to see the Lion and die than to . . . live and not to have seen him."[29]

But Emeth does not die, because he has chosen Aslan without even knowing Aslan. If he had been among those who had come up to the great door and looked Aslan in the face, he would have been among those who chose to enter, because he would have recognized in the face of Aslan what he had been seeking all of his life. If he had been merely religious, or merely sincere, or merely a rule-keeper, he would probably have turned away from that encounter with Aslan. Thus it is to Emeth that Aslan says the crucial words, "All find what they truly seek." Those who truly seek Aslan, though they may not know his name or his true character, will find him in the end, and find joy in being called "Beloved" by the King.[30]

---

29. *The Last Battle*, 155.
30. Ibid., 156.

12

INTERLOCKING STORIES

Why did C.S. Lewis write the Narnia stories? One of his essays, straightforwardly titled "Sometimes Fairy Stories May Say Best What's to be Said," gives us some clues. Part of his reason for writing, he says, was the same as for any writer: a story "bubbles up" in the author's mind and demands to be told. The impulse to write is "very like an itch" that must be scratched.[1]

But, as I suggested earlier, beliefs and stories are inextricably wound together, and all writers will be more or less conscious and deliberate about the beliefs their stories embody. For Lewis, the idea of embodying his Christian beliefs in the stories "pushed itself in of its own accord. It was part of the bubbling." At first it was simply a matter of "seeing pictures in my head. . . . The *Lion* began with a picture of a faun carrying an umbrella and parcels in a snowy wood."[2] But then the Man in Lewis (whom he contrasts with the Author) realized that "stories of this kind could steal past a certain inhibition which had paralyzed much of my own religion in childhood."[3] The trouble had been that the Christian-

---

1. "Sometimes Fairy Stories May Say Best What's to be Said," in *Of This and Other Worlds*, 72.

2. "It all Began with a Picture," in *Of This and Other Worlds*, 79.

3. "Sometimes Fairy Stories May Say Best What's to be Said," 73.

THE SPIRITUALITY OF NARNIA

ity of his youth was (if this does not sound strange) very religious, to be treated with grave seriousness, almost like "something medical." Those inhibitions, which so often stop people thinking clearly about religion and spirituality, were what he called "watchful dragons."

As a result, the Chronicles try to portray Christian faith in an attractive, dragon-avoiding way for people who might be suspicious if it were presented in any other way. The Christian story is what Lewis calls "the hidden story" in the Narnia stories.[4] But because it is hidden, there are more Narnian ways of explaining his purpose: he hopes that we will grow to love Aslan, he hopes that we will want to find Narnia for ourselves, he hopes that we will discover Aslan's other name in our world.

Another way to say this is that Lewis longs for us to join The Great Story, the story of Narnia, the story of our world and of every world—God's Great Story of life, the universe and everything. The reason I think this is the way Lewis plays with the idea of story and with various levels of story throughout the Chronicles—but all with a specific purpose in mind. Let me illustrate.

Early in *The Silver Chair*, Eustace and Jill attend a fine Narnian banquet. As part of the after-dinner entertainment, a blind court musician sings for them "the grand old tale of Prince Cor and Aravis and the horse Bree, which is called *The Horse and His Boy*." Then he adds, tongue in cheek, "I haven't time to tell it now, though it is well worth hearing."[5] Naturally, if the story of Shasta and Bree, Aravis and Hwin, is part of the history of Narnia, it is the kind of story a minstrel would tell. But it is at first confusing, then delightful, to realize that this story is one we already know through reading Lewis' book of the same name.[6] It is as

---

4.   *Letters to Children*, 111.

5.   *The Silver Chair*, 46-47.

6.   *The Voyage of the Dawn Treader*, 36; *The Last Battle*, 85. A similar motif appears in Tolkien's *The Return of the King*, VI:IV, 988-990. Sam Gamgee has expressed a desire to hear a story about his role in the destruction of the Ring: shortly afterwards, a minstrel of Gondor sings "of Frodo of the Nine Fingers and the Ring of Doom." Sam, we are told, "laughed aloud for sheer delight."

though we have somehow managed to hear what this poet has to tell, but we have heard it in our world.

Similarly, in *The Voyage of the Dawn Treader*, Lewis says that if he ever hears how the Lone Islands came to belong to Narnia, "I may put it in some other book." Presumably one of his Narnian friends did tell him, since just such an account appears later in *The Last Battle*. [7]

On another occasion, Lewis seems to be suggesting that he learned the Narnian stories from the lips of the children who went there. Speaking of the scent of the breeze from Aslan's land, he writes: "Edmund and Eustace would never talk about it afterwards. Lucy could only say, 'It would break your heart'." Already this is a little unusual, for Lewis to tell us how the characters felt about an incident afterwards. Usually the stories are told strictly in the character's present tense.

But then an even stranger comment occurs: "Why?" said I, "was it so sad?" "Sad!! No," said Lucy. [8] It is such a short exchange, yet a tantalizing one. Edmund, Eustace and Lucy, apparently, are telling the story of the *Dawn Treader* to Lewis, who simply records it for us. This makes us wonder: how much of the Narnian stories was told to Lewis by the protagonists? Perhaps the story of Eustace the dragon was told to Lewis by Eustace himself? Did Edmund tell him the story of his treachery in the first story? It is an unsettling, destabilizing idea. Our whole understanding of how the stories came into being is thrown into question. Then we realize: no—of course! Lewis is just playing with us. But again for a moment he has removed the barrier between the world of Narnia and its characters, and our own world.

Lewis always had strong feelings about the importance of stories, not least children's stories, [9] and not least because the stories you read

---

7. *The Last Battle*, 85.

8. *The Voyage of the Dawn Treader*, 206.

9. He did not actually like the distinction between children's books and adult books, e.g., "I am almost inclined to set it up as a canon that a children's story which is enjoyed only by children is a bad children's story" ("On Three Ways of Writing for Children," in *Of This and Other Worlds*, 59).

help to make you who you are. If you read the "right kind" of story, it prepares you to deal with many of life's challenges. The Pevensie children, fortunately, have read many of the right books. Thus when they find themselves in the ruins of Cair Paravel at the beginning of *Prince Caspian*, Edmund points out that in adventure books, the children generally find spring of fresh water on the island where they are cast away. Since such stories are reliable, he simply concludes, "We'd better go and look for them."

Or again: if you meet a robin in a strange place, and it seems to be leading you somewhere, should you trust it? Edmund is not sure, but Peter knows the answer: "They're good birds in all the stories I've ever read."[10] Not that the stories always give you the advice you need. Jill reflects wryly that though the stories may tell you that people eat what they kill, "it never tells you what a long, messy job it is plucking and cleaning dead birds, and how cold it makes your fingers."[11] Fortunately, of course, this information, too, is now written in a book that children read, should they ever need to know it—*The Silver Chair.*

For Lewis, however, the purpose of stories is much more than giving practical advice for difficult situations. Digory for one has had his sense of right and wrong, and of natural justice, shaped by the stories he has read. Thus he is confident that Uncle Andrew's mischief will not pay off in the end. He recognizes that Andrew is simply an evil magician "like the ones in the stories." And he warns Andrew that he will get his just desserts in the end, as happens in all the best stories. [12] Digory is looking forward to what Tolkien called "the consolation of fairy stories, the joy of the happy ending."[13]

Uncle Andrew was presumably brought up on those same stories and, though he has traveled a long way from their morality, they still seem to have some purchase on his conscience. As a result Digory's comment

---

10. *The Lion, the Witch and the Wardrobe*, 59.

11. *The Silver Chair*, 76.

12. *The Magician's Nephew*, 28.

13. J. R. R. Tolkien, "On Fairy Stories," in *Tree and Leaf*, 60.

strikes home to his conscience, and for a moment he looks horrified—to such an extent that Digory almost (but not quite) feels sorry for him.[14]

Thus stories help to shape our sense of the world: what is good and what is bad, and how things will work out in the end. As a result, a child who misses out on stories misses out on some of the practicalities of life, but more importantly on what life is all about.

Both of these problems are true of Eustace. He has been raised with books, but not books of stories: "They had a lot to say about exports and imports and governments and drains, but they were weak on dragons."[15] Thus, while a child who had read good stories would know perfectly well that you should never sleep in a dragon's cave on a dragon's hoard, Eustace knows no such thing—and he suffers as a consequence. More importantly, however, when he tries to scratch out in the sand the story of his "dragoning," he cannot do it: because he has not read the right kind of books he "had no idea how to tell a story straight."[16] Reading stories, it seems, gives you models for how you shape your own story and, as a result, make sense of what happens in your life.[17]

Of course, there are grown-ups who do not like stories, but, at least in Lewis' world, they generally have dark reasons for their dislike. King Miraz, for instance, thinks that stories are only for babies, and in his opinion Caspian should be outgrowing them. "At your age you should

---

14.   *The Magician's Nephew,* 28-29.

15.   He is commended later for his bravery in staying the night at Ramandu's table, since "never having read of such a thing . . . it [was] worse for him than for the others" (*The Voyage of the Dawn Treader,* 166-167).

16.   Ibid., 89.

17.   One of Lewis' favourite childhood authors, E. Nesbit, speaks of the importance of stories in the same way. In her first book, for example, the children are trying to decide how they can raise money. Noel says, "Let's read all the books again. We shall get lots of ideas out of them." Their neighbour Albert thinks they are foolish to look for treasure, but "he has not read nearly so many books as we have, so he is very foolish and ignorant" (E. Nesbit, *The Story of the Treasure Seekers* [1899; London: Penguin Books, 1958], 19, 27.

be thinking of battles and adventures, not fairy tales."[18] But of course the stories Caspian has been hearing are precisely those which should—and will—shape his understanding of right and wrong, of who he is and how he needs to behave in the world. They are stories which (accurately) cast Miraz in the role of villain: hence his dislike of them and his efforts to suppress them.

Uncle Andrew similarly, although he is momentarily taken off guard by Digory's vehemence, rejects the stories which speak of evil defeated and right restored. They are all right for children, but really they are no more than "old wives' tales."[19] Tales told by old wives, naturally, cannot be true, so Andrew need not worry. The Dwarf Trumpkin—at least before he meets Aslan—thinks the stories of Aslan similarly old wives' tales. He wishes his leaders would concern themselves more for their practical needs of weapons and food.[20] Little does he realize that it is precisely these old wives' tales which will provide the very victuals and arms he needs—and much more beside, because they are true stories of Aslan, whoever the teller may be.

So far, then, there are two threads to do with story running through the Chronicles. Lewis shows how the Narnian stories interact with one another and with our world. But he also reminds us that good story books will help us shape our own lives, not least in developing our sense of right and wrong. There is yet a third thread to do with story that Lewis adds to this weaving, and it concerns Aslan's name in our world.

When Lucy is in the house of the magician Koriakin on the Island of the Voices, reading through the book of spells, she comes across a story which takes up three pages and tells "about a cup and a sword and a tree and a green hill." She says, "That is the loveliest story I've read or ever shall read in my whole life." Yet as soon as the story is done, she cannot recall it, nor can she turn the pages back. She asks Aslan, "Will you tell

---

18. *Prince Caspian*, 43.
19. *The Magician's Nephew*, 28.
20. *Prince Caspian*, 82.

it to me, Aslan?" And he says, "Indeed, yes. I will tell it to you for years and years."[21]

With the images of cup and sword and tree and hill, and even the number three, Lewis is deliberately making links between Aslan in the Narnia stories and the story of Jesus in the Bible[22]—since all those images are prominent in the biographies of Jesus. He is encouraging us to believe that Lucy will go on (if I may put it this way) learning the story of Jesus from Aslan in our world "for years and years" of her human life. Again, the wall between Narnia and our world has become non-existent.

For Lewis, what binds these three strands of story together is of course Aslan himself. The reason is quite simply that Aslan is the Creator, not only of Narnia but of all worlds, including our own. He guides and oversees all those worlds just as he guides and oversees Narnia, and he oversees their stories, guiding them gently and respectfully towards truth, reality and joy. Whether it is the Narnia tales which connect at their beginning and their end with our world, or the stories of Jesus towards which Aslan nudges the children as they return: all find their larger meaning and fulfillment in Aslan. Even those children's stories which teach us about life are really Aslan stories. Lewis learned this from his friend Tolkien, who believed that all good stories are an echo of The Great Story, God's version of reality, so that, when a story rings true for us, it is because it draws us closer to God's story.[23]

Ancient pagan mythologies are also part of the Great Story. Tolkien did not like the fact that Lewis mixed ideas from different mythologies into the Narnia tales—Father Christmas and fauns, Bacchus and

---

21.   *The Voyage of the Dawn Treader*, 135, 138.

22.   T. S. Eliot (hardly Lewis' favourite poet) makes similar cryptic allusions to the Bible's story of Jesus in "The Journey of the Magi"—"three trees on the low sky" and so on (*Collected Poems 1909-1962* [London: Faber and Faber 1963], 109).

23.   E.g. "The Evangelium [Christian story] has not abrogated legends; it has hallowed them, especially the 'happy ending'" ("On Fairy Stories," 63).

mermaids, and so on.[24] But Lewis did not see these as separate. He believed that all stories are ultimately connected by an underground root system: at some deep level, they interlock.[25] For him, all stories (like the different worlds they describe) are "only spurs jutting out from the great mountains of Aslan."[26] Myth at its best, he writes, is "a real though unfocused gleam of divine truth falling on human imagination."[27] As Shasta observes, "Aslan . . . seems to be at the back of all the stories."[28] Indeed: it is the Creator who holds them all together.

In the New Testament, the book that tells the stories of Jesus and his first followers, one of the writers, Paul, tries to grapple with this matter of Aslan holding all things together:

> From beginning to end, he's there, towering above everything, everyone. So spacious is he, so roomy, that everything of God finds its proper place in him without crowding. Not only that, but all the broken and dislocated pieces of the universe—people and things, animals and atoms—get properly fixed and fit together in vibrant harmonies, all because of his death, his blood that poured down from the cross.[29]

And so for Lewis it was right and fitting that the culminating image at the end of the last of the Chronicles, should be of the next life as a story, The Ultimate Story:

> All their life in this world and all their adventures in Narnia had only been the cover and the title page: now at last they were beginning

---

24. *The Lord of the Rings* is quite different in this respect—a self-contained world with no outside elements of this kind.

25. I suppose the technical word for this is *interpermeability*, but, since Lewis counsels us to "prefer the plain direct word to the long, vague one" (*Letters to Children*, 64) and "ten . . . honest native words . . . [to] one 'literary' word" (*The Letters of C. S. Lewis to Arthur Greeves*, December 4, 1932), I will forbear from using it.

26. *The Last Battle*, 172.

27. *Miracles*, 137-138 (note).

28. *The Horse and His Boy*, 174.

29. *The Letter of Paul to the Colossians*, chapter 1, *The Message*.

Chapter One of the Great Story, which no one on earth has read: which goes on forever: in which every chapter is better than the one before.[30]

---

30.   *The Last Battle*, 173.

13

THROUGH THE WARDROBE

C.S. Lewis does not just want to tell us about people's adventures in Narnia: he also wants to foster in us a longing for Narnia. This longing is that feeling he knew in his own spiritual search which he called joy. He wants us to want Narnia. How does he create that longing? Partly by the simple expedient of making the land of Narnia, the characters, and the adventures, so delicious that we are drawn into it and do not want to leave. As one little girl sobbed after finishing the Chronicles, "I don't want to go on living in this world. I want to live in Narnia with Aslan."[1] I suspect many readers have that kind of reaction—I know I did, and I did not discover the stories until I was thirty—even if we do not express it quite so passionately.

But he also nurtures our desire for Narnia by trying to describe things there, particularly in the new Narnia, running out of words, shrugging his shoulders, and then saying in effect, "Well, you'll just have to experience it for yourself." When he talks about the fruit of Aslan's world, for instance, he despairs of describing it adequately, and encourages us "to get to that country and taste it for yourself."[2] Or,

---

1. *Jack*, 319.
2. *The Last Battle*, 131.

again, he says that things in the Narnian world simply "meant more" than things here, then gives up in despair: "I can't describe it any better than that: if ever you get there you will know what I mean."[3]

And so Lewis' writing (perhaps like all good writing) reaches out from the pages of his books and begins to change the way we think, the way we feel, and even, in this case, what we long for. He wants us to feel that the thing we want more than any other is to be part of the Great Story, which is the story of Narnia and the story of our world and the story of our lives all rolled together. He knew from his own experience and that of his friends Tolkien and Coghill, Dyson and Williams, that it is this Story which makes sense of our lives, which gives us meaning and stability and direction.

But supposing then that we get to the end of the Chronicles, and its magic has so worked on us that we do want to join the Story. What do we do then? Becoming part of a story sounds such an intangible thing. How does one get there?

It is not necessarily easy. Consider, for example, the fact that, in all the stories, getting into Narnia is normally difficult, and sometimes painful, even when people really want to go there. Perhaps the least difficult occasion is the very first, when Lucy simply squeezes through the fur coats and finds herself in an unknown country. Maybe it is not surprising that this would be the experience of Lucy, who is closest in spirit to Aslan.[4] When the four children first go through the wardrobe together, however, they have a sense of being pursued there, and it is hardly pleasant. They find that, wherever they turn, Mrs. Macready with her party of tourists seems about to intrude on them, until the only resort

---

3.   Ibid., 162.

4.   Of course, Edmund also arrives easily, though at this point he is hardly in tune with Aslan: perhaps Lewis had simply not developed this motif yet. The other painless arrival is that of Helen, first queen of Narnia, who arrives there "quickly, simply and sweetly as a bird flies to its nest," but we know little of her story or character (*The Magician's Nephew*, 127).

left to them is to hide in the wardrobe. They felt as if "some magic in the house had come to life and was chasing them into Narnia."[5]

On other occasions also, entering Narnia is quite traumatic. At the beginning of *The Voyage of the Dawn Treader*, for example, Edmund, Lucy and Eustace are tossed unceremoniously into the ocean, where they seem in danger of drowning until Caspian rescues them. Then, in *Prince Caspian*, they are tugged into Narnia with "a most frightful pulling" and cries of "Ow!" and "Oh!" and "Ugh!"[6] When *The Silver Chair* opens, Jill and Eustace are desperately trying to escape from the school bullies, and cry out for Aslan's help. The most violent of all, of course, is in *The Last Battle*, when the children, their parents, and the Professor and Polly are all catapulted into Narnia (or, in some cases, Aslan's world) by a train crash in which they are killed. None of these is a happy experience.

I suspect the kind of pain and difficulty which attends travel to Narnia is a warning of what happens when we respond to the call of joy. We want it—of course we want it, more than anything else, that is the point—but there is a price to be paid. As in Lewis' case, to follow the call of joy can lead to a kind of conversion, and to be converted is almost never easy. After all, to get married after a life of singleness (as Lewis did) is a kind of conversion that causes trepidation (at the very least) to many. To renounce citizenship of one country and to become a citizen of a new land (as refugees often do) is an emotionally difficult conversion. Lewis himself recognized such parallels in a letter to someone who had recently entered the Story:

> [W]hatever people who have never undergone an adult conversion
> may say, it is a process not without its distresses. Indeed they are
> the very sign of a true initiation. Like learning to swim or to skate,

---

5. *The Lion, the Witch and the Wardrobe*, 52.
6. *Prince Caspian*, 12.

or getting married or taking up a profession. There are cold shudderings about all these processes.[7]

Spiritual conversion can be painful, whether from (say) atheism to Christianity (like Lewis) or indeed from Christianity to atheism. Often we find in ourselves emotional resistance to the change. After all, we are leaving behind a world which is familiar for one that (however attractive) is new and daunting. It normally means a change of worldview, of community and of lifestyle. There is tension between the old reality and the new reality. We find internal resistance, even when the change is something we want, and often we need a push. Some religious communities talk about conversion as being "born again": in spite of the negative cultural connotations, it is a powerful and often appropriate image.[8]

Of course, there are two sides to getting into Narnia. On the one hand, there is the matter of the individual's choice. At the beginning of *The Voyage of the Dawn Treader,* Edmund and Lucy are looking longingly at a painting of the *Dawn Treader.* In the first scene of *The Silver Chair,* Eustace and Jill cry out to get into Narnia. When the train crash occurs in *The Last Battle,* the children have been trying to find the magic rings so they can go back into Narnia.

But this is not the whole picture. As all the books make clear, there is a second will involved in the whole process. Thus the children feel "chased" into the wardrobe in the first book. Edmund, Lucy and Eustace are sucked helplessly into the painting of the *Dawn Treader.* The final train crash is outside their control. Someone else is taking the initiative. "You would not have called to me unless I had been calling to you."[9] Once again there is a mysterious intermingling between what Aslan wants and

---

7. *Letters of C.S. Lewis,* 419.

8. Indeed, Freudians have been known to speculate that the wardrobe with its fur coats is an image of the birth canal: "[S]ome will be tempted . . . to see in this tale of a world which is reached through a dark hole surrounded by fur coats [an] unconscious image of the passage through which Lewis first entered the world from his mother's body" (A.N. Wilson, 228).

9. *The Silver Chair,* 28.

what people from our world want—and Aslan is interested in us long before we are interested in him. Edmund is getting at this when Eustace asks him, "Do you know [Aslan]?" and he replies, "Well—he knows me."[10] It is from beginning to end Aslan's idea that the children should get involved in the world of Narnia, and should get to know him.

I suspect that in many types of conversion there is a sense that what is happening is not entirely the convert's own decision. Marriage after all is a decision of two people, not just one; and often those involved have a sense of fate or of being "made for one another." Normally refugees have limited choices and feel driven to leave their own country and to find a new home.

The paradox of our freedom and Aslan's pursuit was present in Lewis' own experience. On the one hand he says of his choice (on top of the bus) to "open, to unbuckle" to spiritual reality:

> I was offered what now appears a moment of wholly free choice. In a sense. . . . I am . . . inclined to think that this came nearer to being a perfectly free act than most that I have ever done.

On the other hand, he says of that same experience: "I say 'I chose,' yet it did not really seem possible to do the opposite."[11] And certainly when he finally "admitted that God was God," there was a sense of unwillingly facing the inevitable, "the steady, unrelenting approach of Him whom I so earnestly desired not to meet."[12] Both aspects are present, and both are real.

This is not just a philosophical conundrum, however. Think of it this way: if we find ourselves wanting to join the Great Story, we can take heart since in all likelihood we feel that way because Aslan is already calling us to do so. That immediately increases the likelihood that we will get there!

---

10. *The Voyage of the Dawn Treader*, 97.
11. *Surprised by Joy*, 179.
12. Ibid., 182.

On our side of the transaction, it seems to me that Lewis gives us three practical things we can do. Firstly, we can take joy more seriously. I almost said, "we can pursue joy," but Lewis is clear that it is not be found that way. It sneaks up on us when we least expect it. But just because it is elusive we should not therefore shrug it off or make light of it or dismiss it by "calling it names like Nostalgia and Romanticism and Adolescence."[13] It is true that joy is not everybody's way through the wardrobe,[14] but for those of us who have loved the Chronicles, it seems likely that it is because we resonate with its language of joy. So we need to take it seriously.

Where we find joy, of course, will vary. Lewis offers us many possibilities. We may find joy in the beauties of nature (as he did at a young age), or in stories that contain far-off echoes of the Great Story (as the adolescent Lewis did). It may be in a dream with "a lovely meaning too lovely to put into words, which makes the dream so beautiful that you remember it all your life and are always wishing you could get into that dream again" (as when the Pevensies first hear the name of Aslan).[15] For some it may be "the feeling you have when you wake up in the morning and realize that it is the beginning of the holidays" (as Lucy did)[16], or "a fresh, wild, lonely smell that [seems] to get into your brain and [makes] you feel that you could go up mountains at a run or wrestle with an elephant" (as the crew of the *Dawn Treader* felt).[17]

---

13. "The Weight of Glory," in *Screwtape Proposes a Toast*, 97.

14. *Mere Christianity*, for example, works on a different premise: that once we understand that there is an objective standard of right and wrong, built by the Creator into the structure of the world, we will realize that we have fallen short of that standard, and will look for a way to set things straight. I suspect that fewer people these days will enter by this door than by the joy door.

15. *The Lion, the Witch and the Wardrobe*, 65.

16. Ibid., 65.

17. *The Voyage of the Dawn Treader*, 201

In his most famous sermon, "The Weight of Glory," one of his most moving treatments of the subject, Lewis seems to assume that we all have a yearning for joy, even if we fail to recognize or honour it:

> In speaking of this desire for our own far-off country . . . I feel
> a certain shyness. I am almost committing an indecency. I am
> trying to rip open the inconsolable secret in each one of you . . .
> the secret . . . which pierces with such sweetness that when, in very
> intimate conversation, the mention of it becomes imminent, we
> grow awkward and affect to laugh at ourselves. . . . We cannot hide
> it because our experience is constantly suggesting it, and we betray
> ourselves like lovers at the mention of a name.[18]

The important thing is to realize that the tugs of joy are not an end in themselves, "not the wave but the wave's imprint on the sand"[19], merely "good images of what we really desire. . . . the scent of a flower we have not found, the echo of a tune we have not heard, news from a country we have never yet visited."[20] We need to follow along the way these signposts are pointing us, which leads to "the naked Other," who, for some time, Lewis avoided referring to by the obvious term, "God."[21]

The second thing I notice in Lewis about joining the Story is the encouragement to a kind of surrender. In his own life, the circumstances were perfectly mundane: he was on a bus going up Headington Hill in Oxford:

> I could open the door or keep it shut; I could unbuckle the armour
> or keep it on. . . . I chose to open, to unbuckle, to loosen the rein.[22]

In fictional terms, maybe the closest analogy is with Eustace's undragoning in *The Voyage of the Dawn Treader*. However much he wishes to

---

18. "The Weight of Glory," 97.
19. *Surprised by Joy*, 175.
20. "The Weight of Glory," 98.
21. *Surprised by Joy*, 176-177.
22. Ibid., 179.

tear his scaly skin off, he cannot do it. Only Aslan can do it, and Eustace's role is simply to surrender. With what seems almost to be sexual imagery, Eustace says:

> "Then the lion said . . . You will have to let me undress you. . . . So I
> just lay flat down on my back to let him do it."[23]

Certainly mystics speak of their relationship with God in quasi-sexual terms, and Lewis was familiar with their writings, so maybe these overtones are intentional.

Lewis' main point, however, seems to be that in our spiritual searching there is a limit to how far we can get by ourselves. But, if he is right, behind our longing for joy is a supernatural Being who is more interested in our search than we are. And at a certain point, better sooner than later, it is good to acknowledge that reality, and (however we may want to conceive of it) to surrender to the real Aslan. That will make our progress much faster.

The last clue Lewis offers as to how we enter the Story is his repeated references to the identity of Aslan in our world. Like Lucy, we are offered the chance to learn from Aslan "for years and years," the stories about him which involve "a cup and a sword and a tree and a green hill."[24] For Lewis, learning the identity of Jesus was the last step in his movement towards faith along the pathway marked out by joy. This was not a rejection of joy, nor of the mythologies where he had often tasted joy, but a fulfillment of their promise. Tolkien expressed the connection this way:

> The Gospels [the stories of Jesus] contain a fairy-story, or a story of
> a larger kind *which embraces all the essence of fairy-stories.* . . . But
> this story has entered History . . . This story is supreme; and it is true.

---

23.   *The Voyage of the Dawn Treader*, 96.
24.   Ibid., 135, 138.

Art has been verified. God is the Lord, of angels, and of men—and of elves. Legend and history have met and fused.[25]

We too are invited to explore these stories, as Lewis did, and find the reality of Aslan in our world.

Ultimately, the success of Lewis' Narnia Chronicles can best be measured by the criterion he himself gives us: do the Chronicles help circumvent the watchful dragons and enable us to discover for ourselves what was for Lewis the ultimate source of joy? Only the reader can answer that question.

---

25.   "On Fairy Stories", 62-63 (italics original).